Rediscovering
Wonderland

Rediscovering Wonderland

THE EXPEDITION THAT LAUNCHED YELLOWSTONE NATIONAL PARK

M. MARK MILLER

TWODOT®

GUILFORD, CONNECTICUT
HELENA, MONTANA

This book is dedicated to Rachel Phillips, the research director of the Gallatin History Museum. Rachel is always ready with a smile to dig out information, maps, or photos for anyone who asks, even me.

A · TWODOT® · BOOK

An imprint of Globe Pequot, the trade division of
The Rowman & Littlefield Publishing Group, Inc.
4501 Forbes Blvd., Ste. 200
Lanham, MD 20706
www.rowman.com

Distributed by NATIONAL BOOK NETWORK

British Library Cataloguing in Publication Information available

Library of Congress Cataloging-in-Publication Data
Names: Miller, M. Mark, author.
Title: Rediscovering wonderland : the expedition that launched Yellowstone
    National Park / M. Mark Miller.
Other titles: Expedition that launched Yellowstone National Park
Description: Guilford, Connecticut : TwoDot, [2022] | Includes bibliographical references and
    index. | Summary: "A history of the exploration and founding of America's first national park"—
    Provided by publisher.
Identifiers: LCCN 2021035733 (print) | LCCN 2021035734 (ebook) | ISBN 9781493060740
    (paperback) | ISBN 9781493060757 (epub)
Subjects: LCSH: Yellowstone National Park—Discovery and exploration. | Washburn Expedition
    (1870)—History. | Yellowstone National Park—History.
Classification: LCC F722 .M55 2022 (print) | LCC F722 (ebook) | DDC 978.7/52—dc23
LC record available at https://lccn.loc.gov/2021035733
LC ebook record available at https://lccn.loc.gov/2021035734

CONTENTS

Map vi

Preface vii

Chapter One: Mountain Men Get No Respect 1

Chapter Two: Recruiting Good Men 15

Chapter Three: Into the Wilderness 31

Chapter Four: Falls and Canyons 45

Chapter Five: Everts Gets Lost 59

Chapter Six: Everts's Ordeal 71

Chapter Seven: Searching for Everts 85

Chapter Eight: Geyserland and Home 97

Chapter Nine: Persuading the World 111

Chapter Ten: Superintendent Langford 123

Chapter Eleven: Fame and Obscurity 139

Notes 147

References 157

Index 161

About the Author 168

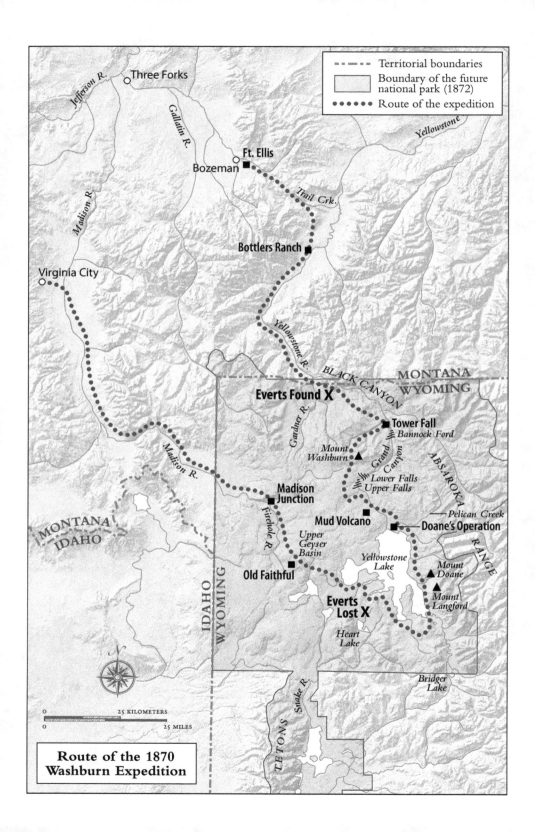

Three Forks

Jefferson R.

Gallatin R.

Yellowstone

Ft. Ellis

Bozeman

Trail Crk.

Madison R.

Bottlers Ranch

Virginia City

Yellowstone R.

BLACK CANYON

MONTANA

WYOMING

Everts Found **X**

Gardner R.

Tower Fall

Bannock Ford

Mount Washburn ▲

Grand Canyon

ABSAROKA

Madison R.

Lower Falls
Upper Falls

Madison Junction

MONTANA

IDAHO

Firehole R.

Mud Volcano

Pelican Creek

Doane's Operation

RANGE

Upper Geyser Basin

Yellowstone Lake

Mount Doane ▲

Old Faithful

IDAHO

WYOMING

Everts Lost **X**

▲ Mount Langford

Heart Lake

Bridger Lake

N

Snake R.

0   25 KILOMETERS

0   25 MILES

TETONS

Route of the 1870 Washburn Expedition

PREFACE

On August 17, 1870, nineteen men of the Washburn Expedition rode out of a camp near Fort Ellis, east of Bozeman, Montana, on their way to the wilderness that was to become Yellowstone Park. Later, two of those men, Nathaniel P. Langford and Gustavus Cheney Doane, would claim to be the discoverers of the park. Langford, who has been called "the spark plug" of the expedition, titled his book about the trip *The Discovery of Yellowstone Park*.[1] When he died in 1909, newspapers across the United States lauded him as "The Discoverer of Yellowstone Park." Doane, the lieutenant who commanded the Army unit that escorted the expedition, later claimed he was entitled to be park superintendent "by right of discovery." He died on May 5, 1892, with little fanfare.

The veracity of the two men's claims depend on the definition of *discovery*. Native Americans knew about the wonders of the area at the headwaters of the Yellowstone and Madison Rivers for millennia, and the same was true for Euro-Americans for decades. But by definitions that are still in force today, credit for discovery belongs not to the first person to see something but to the first person to publish credible observations of it. Native people's experiences never count, and verbal reports by working-class people, like fur trappers and gold prospectors, are given little credit.

Even by those standards, it's hard to claim that the park area was not discovered before the 1870 expedition that was named for its elected leader, General Henry Dana Washburn. Mountain men's stories about spouting geysers, deep canyons, and a huge mountain lake had been printed in newspapers scattered across the country. A cartographer for the Montana Territory surveyor general's office had published a map showing those things. Two men who had seen them just a year before were getting their story published in a national magazine. Members of the Washburn Expedition knew about all of those things. They had heard talks by the men on the 1869 trip and took copies of the cartographer's map with them. In fact, the Washburn Expedition was launched because the wonders of the area were known—not because they were waiting to be "discovered."

Gustavus Cheney Doane commanded the Army escort that accompanied the Washburn Expedition. He devoted his life to earning fame as an explorer.

The late nineteenth century was a time when people could garner fame and fortune for reports of things that surely existed whether human eyes had seen them or not, such as the headwaters of the Nile and Amazon Rivers and the North and South Poles. People who made arduous trips to see such things and published reports about them were credited with their discovery and subsequently became heroes. The wonders of Yellowstone were perfect candidates for glory hunters. Langford and Doane were such men.

This is not to say that the Washburn Expedition wasn't important, but its contribution was in documenting the features of the area and publicizing them, not in discovery. The expedition included prominent Montana citizens whose descriptions could not be dismissed as tall tales like those of trappers and prospectors. Equally important, several of the men on the expedition were skilled writers who had the connections to get their accounts published in a timely manner.

The publicity generated by the Washburn Expedition placed the park area in Americans' consciousness and helped persuade the US Congress to reserve it "for the enjoyment of the people" by creating the world's first national park.

By the 1870s, most of the land in the contiguous forty-eight states had been explored and mapped. That even included the formidable Grand Canyon of the Colorado. John Wesley Powell had led a boating expedition through the canyon in 1869. About the only large section of the country that remained unexplored was an area lying southeast of the point where the borders of Wyoming, Idaho, and Montana meet—the area that was to become Yellowstone National Park.

Towering mountains that were thrown up eons ago by eruptions of a super volcano surround the headwaters of the Yellowstone and Madison Rivers, where the spectacular wonders are. Access to them was only through rugged river canyons, and hostile Indians guarded access to those canyons. The area is buried under a thick blanket of snow for much of the year. It's no wonder that fur trappers and gold prospectors avoided the area until after they searched more accessible places.

Mountain man brigades began regularly trapping in the park area in the 1820s and continued there until the bottom fell out of the beaver trade in the 1840s. After that, visits were rare until the 1860s, when gold was discovered nearby in Montana. Then prospector expeditions forced their way into the area to scour every stream and gully for gold.

The prospectors brought reports of the wonders they had seen, such as fountains of boiling water hundreds of feet high, canyons a thousand feet deep, and a mountaintop lake that covered a hundred square miles. Such reports were so extreme that they reminded people of tall tales told by mountain men decades before. But by the mid-1860s, the stories had come from so many sources and were so consistent that people began to believe that there really must be wonders in the area. It was time for an expedition of credible observers to explore the area and report back what was really there.

REDISCOVERING WONDERLAND IS BASED ON A RICH VEIN OF FIRST-PERSON accounts of the Washburn Expedition. The most extensive account is N. P. Langford's book, which was published in 1905 with two titles: *The Discovery of Yellowstone Park* on its cover and *Diary of the Washburn Expedition to the Yellowstone and Firehole Rivers in the Year 1870* on its title page. Both titles are misleading—the first because it claims credit for "discovery" when the area was well known to Native Americans and to Euro-Americans, the second because the book is not a diary but a reminiscence Langford constructed from notes taken on the trip and other sources. Everyone is a hero in the stories they tell about themselves, and doubtless Langford embellishes the importance of his role, but his account provides a detailed, day-by-day account of the expedition.

As soon as the Washburn Expedition exited the park area on September 22, 1870, Langford rushed ahead of the group to the nearest telegraph office to tell editors at the *Helena Herald*. The *Herald* published a short article based on his notes, but he left it to his companions to write accounts for the territorial newspapers and reserved his effort for national media.

On September 23, the *Herald* published an article two columns long under the headline "Interesting Data of the Trip, From Notes Furnished by Hon. N. P. Langford." Somebody, perhaps Langford himself, also sent the news to the *New Northwest*, a newspaper in Deer Lodge, Montana, which also published an article on September 23.

That started a steady stream of news stories in Montana newspapers, several of them written by expedition members who were skillful writers. General Washburn provided the first article by a member of the expedition, and Cornelius Hedges, who was a writer for the *Herald*, wrote a four-part series of long pieces and sent an article to an Iowa newspaper. As was common practice at the time, newspapers across Montana and the United States republished accounts from other newspapers.

LANGFORD WAS AIMING FOR BIGGER EDITORIAL TARGETS. NEARLY A YEAR after the expedition headed to the park area, *Scribner's Monthly*, a leading national magazine of the time, published a two-part series by Langford titled "The Wonders of the Yellowstone." *Scribner's* was so prominent that newspapers printed summaries of its contents and stimulated nationwide interest in the park area.

Langford's brightly written articles described Montana and the park area in glowing terms and claimed that when Northern Pacific Railroad reached the area "thousands of tourists will be attracted to both Montana and Wyoming in order to behold with their own eyes the wonders here described."[2]

As the son of a US senator, twenty-four-year-old Walter Trumbull had the connections to get his account of the expedition published in a prominent magazine, the *Overland Monthly*, in May 1871.

News about Truman Everts, who strayed away from the expedition and couldn't be found, kept the story alive. On October 7 newspapers reported that Warren Gillette, who had stayed behind to search for Everts, had returned to civilization without success. On October 27, the *Herald* reported that Yellowstone Jack Baronett and George Pritchett had rescued Everts, setting off another round of news stories across Montana and the nation.

News about Everts stimulated great interest in newspapers across the nation. In November 1871, *Scribner's* published Everts's colorful account of his ordeal under the title "Thirty-Seven Days of Peril." Everts's story must be taken with the proverbial grain of salt. He describes conversations with ghosts and his arms and legs that probably were due to starvation-induced hallucinations. Nonetheless, it's a compelling story.

Lieutenant Gustavus Cheney Doane, who commanded the Army escort for the expedition, also provided an extensive day-by-day account of it. Doane, who was under orders to provide a report of his observations to the secretary of war, was formal and dry in places. But Doane was a skilled observer and writer who often painted graphic verbal pictures of what he saw and described the expedition's daily activities.

Other important sources for *Rediscovering Wonderland* are diaries that weren't published until decades later. Doubtless, Cornelius Hedges intended his diary just to be used for his newspaper stories, and *Contributions to the Historical Society of Montana* didn't publish it until 1904. Warren Gillette never wrote an account of the trip. His journal wasn't published until 1972 in *Montana, the Magazine of Western History.*[3]

THERE IS NO FICTION IN THIS BOOK. NO NAMES HAVE BEEN CHANGED, NO characters have been invented, and no events have been fabricated. These stories adhere to the facts as they can be documented or reasonably inferred. They come primarily from first-person accounts by the people who lived the adventure.

Anything enclosed in quotation marks here comes from material written by the person being quoted (or by people the authors quoted). Of course the direct quotations are the reconstructions of their authors.

Writing about the area that became Yellowstone Park before the park was created presents challenges to writers who want to be precise. Nathaniel P. Langford claimed credit for finding something before it existed in name when he titled his book *The Discovery of Yellowstone Park 1870.* To avoid confusion, I have called the region visited by the Washburn Expedition "the park area" or "Wonderland" until the events of 1872, when it was officially designated a national park.

Throughout, I have used place names as they are recognized now so today's readers can determine where the actions took place. However, I have tried to describe geothermal and geological features as they appeared in 1870. For example, Mud Volcano was hurling gobs of mud in 1870 but is now a quiet spring.

Authors have called the exploration described in this book by several names depending upon whom they thought should receive credit for its accomplishments. These include "The Washburn Expedition," "The Washburn-Doane Expedition," and "The Washburn-Doane-Langford Expedition." For sake of economy, I have chosen to refer to it simply as "The Washburn Expedition."

Chroniclers of the expedition were quite aware of social distinctions, and when they referred to "the expedition," they generally meant only the nine government officials and entrepreneurs who took the trip, not including the two packers and two cooks they hired. Members of the Army escort that accompanied the group bivouacked separately and also weren't considered part of the expedition. I retain these distinctions and call the entire group "the explorers."

While preparing this book, I consulted a number of secondary sources and occasionally found errors in them, but I decided to leave it to historians to correct the record. Nitpicking details invites scrutiny, and I am painfully aware of how easy it is to make mistakes. Despite the efforts of me and my editors, errors always creep in. Of course I take responsibility for any mistakes that remain.

CHAPTER ONE

Mountain Men Get No Respect

ALTHOUGH HUNDREDS, PERHAPS THOUSANDS, OF MEN PASSED THROUGH the area that was to become Yellowstone National Park before 1870, it remained officially undiscovered. No government expedition had managed to penetrate the ten-thousand-foot-high mountains that surrounded the area. There were no official reports showing the wonders there, so officially they didn't exist.

Of course the geysers, waterfalls, canyons, and petrified forests had been there for eons. They just hadn't been reported in a way that penetrated the public consciousness. People usually dismissed as tall tales the oral reports of trappers and prospectors who visited the area. The few written descriptions were in private hands or published in obscure newspapers and government reports. But by the late 1860s, persuasive evidence had accumulated: There were wonders that remained to be definitively documented at the headwaters of the Yellowstone and Madison Rivers.

Rumors of wonders at those headwaters had circulated around Montana for decades, but they were usually dismissed as the exaggerations of mountain men who had visited the area for more than sixty years. Mountain men had a tradition of spinning fanciful tales for their amusement, and that may have prompted skepticism about reports of things they had actually seen. Nobody could be expected to believe accounts of a canyon that was a thousand feet deep, a mountaintop lake that covered a hundred square miles, or fountains that spouted boiling water hundreds of feet into the air.

Reports of gold prospectors who had scoured the park area beginning in the 1860s also were greeted with skepticism. Like the mountain men, most prospectors were neither well educated nor skilled writers. Skepticism was so severe that when Charles Cook returned to Helena after touring the area with two companions in 1869, he was reluctant to talk in public about what he had seen. Cook was invited to tell about his trip to a group of citizens in the directors room at First National Bank in Helena, but when he discovered there were many people in the room he didn't know, he was unwilling to speak for fear of risking his reputation for honesty.

Cook and one of his companions, David Folsom, co-wrote an article describing their trip, but they had difficulty getting it published. *Scribner's Monthly*, a prestigious magazine with a national circulation, and the *New York Herald* declined to publish the article because "they had a reputation they could not risk with such unreliable material."[1] The *Western Monthly*, a smaller and less prestigious magazine, finally accepted the article and published it in July 1870, just weeks before the Washburn Expedition departed.[2] The *Western Monthly* edited Cook and Folsom's article so severely that it didn't provide much information about the route their trip took.

The first Euro-American to see Yellowstone's wonders was John Colter, who went there in the winter of 1807-08 looking for Indian trading partners. Colter had been a member of the famous Lewis and Clark Expedition that explored the American West beginning in 1803. He came within a hundred miles of what is now the park in 1806 when he accompanied William Clark on his return trip down the Yellowstone River.

When the Corps of Discovery got back to the confluence of the Yellowstone and Missouri Rivers, Colter sought permission to muster out so he could return upriver with a pair of trappers. After Lewis and Clark extracted a promise from the rest of their men that they wouldn't seek similar treatment, the captains acceded to Colter's request.

Colter soon joined Manuel Lisa's Missouri Fur Company, and Lisa sent Colter up the Yellowstone River to make friends with Crow Indians and bring them back to his trading post. While on this mission, Colter passed through parts of what is now Yellowstone National Park.

In 1810, Colter returned to Saint Louis and told his old boss, William Clark, what he had seen. Clark used Colter's descriptions and included the locations of hot springs and Yellowstone Lake and Falls for a map he published in 1814.[3]

Colter, who apparently was illiterate, didn't leave a written description of his adventures, but they were recorded by several prominent writers, including Washington Irving. Now Colter is usually credited with being the first white man to see the park area's wonders and often is called their "discoverer."

The War of 1812 stalled the beaver trade between the United States and

Europe. When the war ended in 1815, trapping resumed. Beaver must have been abundant in the early 1800s when trappers first arrived in places like the headwaters of the Missouri where the Madison, Jefferson, and Gallatin Rivers run together. Each of those rivers had its own tributaries that provided ideal beaver habitat. But soon, heavy trapping made beaver scarce along the easily accessible rivers, so trappers pushed into more remote places. By the 1820s, trappers had forced their way through the mountains that barricaded Yellowstone's wonders.

The first written description of geysers on the Upper Yellowstone by someone who actually saw them was in a letter a fur trapper named Daniel T. Potts sent to his brother in 1827. In his letter, which was published in a Philadelphia newspaper, Potts described "a large fresh water lake on the very top of the mountain, which is almost one hundred by forty miles in diameter, and as clear as crystal."[4] Potts added, "On the south border of this lake is a number of hot and boiling springs some of water and others of most beautiful fine clay and resembles that of a mush pot and throws its particles to the immense height of twenty to 30 feet."[5] Potts was describing Yellowstone Lake and the West Thumb Geyser Basin.

About 1829, a nineteen-year-old trapper named Joe Meek was camped along the Gallatin River in southwest Montana with a brigade of mountain men when Blackfeet Indians attacked. Meek escaped and made his way over high mountains to a spot where he saw "the whole country beyond was smoking with the vapor from boiling springs, and burning with hot gasses, issuing from small craters each of which was emitting a sharp whistling sound."[6] Apparently, Meek had found what is now called Norris Geyser Basin.

In the 1840s, Meek moved to Oregon, where he helped organize the territorial government. In the 1860s, historian Frances Fuller Victor interviewed Meek several times and wrote a book about his adventures, but it wasn't published until 1870, too late to have any impact on the Washburn Expedition.

A clerk for the American Fur Company, Warren Angus Ferris, heard about the grand geysers in Yellowstone's Upper Geyser Basin at a mountain man rendezvous in 1833. The next year he decided to see them for himself. After riding hard for two days, Ferris camped after dark near the bank of the Firehole River. Despite fatigue, Ferris said, "the continual roaring of the springs" kept him awake and filled his "slumbers with visions of waterspouts, cataracts, fountains, jets d'eau of immense dimensions, etc. etc."

The next morning Ferris got up to find "clouds of vapor seemed like a dense fog to overhang the springs from which frequent reports or explosions of different loudness constantly assailed our ears." Ferris also clearly saw geysers, "columns of water of various dimensions projected high in the air, accompanied by loud explosions and sulfurous vapors."[7]

Ferris's account of what he saw was published in the Buffalo, New York, *Western Literary Messenger* in 1842 and reprinted the same year in the Nauvoo, Illinois, *Wasp*. The publications were obscure, and Ferris's descriptions were not well known until the twentieth century.

In the years between 1830 and 1843, a trapper named Osborne Russell kept a journal describing his adventures in the northwest frontier. Russell's journal provides one of the earliest first-person, written accounts of travel to the Upper Yellowstone. He apparently didn't know the word *geyser*, but Russell described what he called "Hour Spring" this way: "The first thing that attracts the attention is a hole about fifteen inches in diameter in which water is boiling slowly about four inches below the surface. At length it begins to boil and bubble violently and the water commences raising and shooting upward until the column arises to a height of sixty feet. It falls to the ground in drops on a circle of about thirty feet in diameter being perfectly cold when it strikes the ground. It continues shooting up in this manner five or six minutes and then sinks back to its former state of slowly boiling for an hour—and then shoots forth as before."[8] Apparently the geyser Russell described no longer exists. He rewrote his journal for publication, but that didn't happen until 1914, when his nephew put it out in a highly edited version. Russell's book has been republished several times.[9]

In the 1840s, the beaver trade collapsed because fashion in men's hats changed from beaver to silk after trade opened with China. Also, trappers had decimated the beaver population, so it was hard to make a fortune selling pelts. A few trappers stayed in the area living nomadic lives and earning enough for the essentials like gunpowder, coffee, and sugar. They took Indian wives and subsisted on fish and game and had what the Earl of Dunraven called "a Delicious Life."[10] Others joined the great land rush to Oregon Territory, where some became prominent citizens. A few began buying spent oxen from Oregon-bound settlers in Idaho and taking them to Montana, where the animals regained their strength in the grass-rich valleys. The next year, they were taken back to Idaho and traded, one refreshed animal for two exhausted ones.

Conventional wisdom holds that trapper accounts of what they saw in the park were generally dismissed as tall tales. It's true that mountain men told stories to entertain themselves and each other around their campfires and invented preposterous events to see how far they could go before gullible recruits would doubt them. Jim Bridger was the most famous teller of tall tales. One of his favorites was a story of being chased up a box canyon by a hundred Indians. He would say he discovered there was no escape and pause. When someone finally asked what happened next, he would reply, "Why, I was killed."

Bridger also told about seeing a magnificent bull elk standing on a hilltop. He said he raised his gun and shot, but the animal continued to pose. Bridger tried again, and the elk still stood. Bridger's explanation: He was looking through a mountain of crystal-clear glass that magnified the image of an elk that was miles away. Bridger also told about a petrified forest where petrified birds sat on the petrified branches of petrified trees singing petrified songs, and of a stream where fish swam freely across the Continental Divide.

Preposterous as these stories seem, they are all just exaggerations. Bridger projected himself into the story of his mountain man friend Jedidiah Smith, who was killed by pursuing Indians in a box canyon. Obsidian cliff, although far from crystal clear, is a mountain of glass. The park area contains several petrified forests, and at the Two Ocean Pass south of the current park boundary, fish swim across the Continental Divide.

A motivation for mountain men's tall tales was probably that when they told true stories about such things as the Grand Canyon of the Yellowstone and the Upper Geyser Basin, nobody believed them. When Jim Bridger returned to live out his old age in Missouri, a newspaper there refused to publish his accounts of things he actually had seen. Men like Bridger probably decided that if people wouldn't believe their factual reports, they might as well have fun exaggerating.

The fact that trappers told tales that many people discounted isn't the whole story. US Army officers often praised Bridger's encyclopedic knowledge of western geography and hired him as a scout.

As early as 1852, Lieutenant John W. Gunnison of the US Army Corps of Topographical Engineers praised Bridger's descriptions of the headwaters of the Yellowstone where "A lake sixty miles long,[11] cold and pellucid, lies embosomed amid high precipitous mountains. On the west side is a sloping plain several miles wide, with clumps of trees and groves of pine. The ground resounds to the tread of horses. Geysers spout up seventy feet high, with a terrific hissing noise, at regular intervals. Waterfalls are sparkling, leaping, and thundering down the precipices, and collect in the pool below."[12] Gunnison's account of Bridger's descriptions was published in an obscure book titled *The History of the Mormons*, so it was not obvious that it reported Yellowstone wonders.

In 1859, the Army ordered Captain William F. Raynolds to look for a route between the drainages of the Yellowstone and Missouri Rivers, but he went too early in the spring of 1860 and couldn't get through mountain passes choked with snow. In his report, Raynolds wrote, "Had our attempt to enter this district been made a month later in the season, the snow would have mainly disappeared, and there would have been no insurmountable obstacles to overcome. I cannot doubt, therefore, that at no very distant day the mysteries of this region will be fully revealed, and though small in extent, I regard the valley of the upper Yellowstone as the most interesting unexplored district in our widely expanded country."

Raynolds hired Jim Bridger as his guide and believed the mountain man's accounts of the park area. After failing his mission, Raynolds said, "We were compelled to content ourselves with listening to marvelous tales of burning plains, immense lakes, and boiling springs, without being able to verify these wonders."[13]

Raynolds's official report included Bridger's descriptions of the park area, but the Civil War delayed its publication until 1868. Still, it shows that responsible people believed Bridger's accounts of marvels at the headwaters of the Yellowstone and Madison Rivers.

Of course not all trappers had Jim Bridger's reputation, and their tales were met with skepticism. Emma Cowan's description of such tales is typical. She recalled that when she was a girl in Virginia City, Montana, in the 1860s, her father brought a man home to tell stories to his family.[14]

Emma said, "My father termed them fish stories. However, I enjoyed them immensely. My fairy books could not equal such wonderful tales. Fountains of boiling water, crystal clear, thrown hundreds of feet in the air, only to fall back into cups of their own forming; pools of water within whose limpid depths tints of the various rainbows were reflected; mounds and terraces of gaily colored sand—these and many others were the tales unfolded.

Although we enjoyed his stories, for he told them well, they were considered by me, even as by others, merely the phantasy of his imagination."[15]

One reason the Yellowstone Park area remained off the public mind until the 1870s is that reports of the wonders there remained in private hands or were published in obscure journals. It wasn't until years after the park was established that historians uncovered many of the mountain men's written accounts of their adventures and Army surveyors' secondhand reports of what they found credible.

Certainly, mountain men's stories of the things they had seen often were dismissed as tall tales, but there are other reasons such accounts weren't taken seriously. Mountain men visited the park area mostly from 1820 to 1840. That was before transportation had developed, so it took months for trappers to return back east and tell their stories. By that time, they were reporting stale news. Also, mass-circulation newspapers and magazines had yet to develop their voracious appetite for reports of the new and unusual. Of course there were no newspapers in the Rocky Mountain West then to collect accounts and no telegraph lines to distribute them.

All of this had changed by the 1860s, when plans to explore the park area became common. By then, the first transcontinental railroad had been built and a second was planned to cross Montana. Telegraph lines moved information back and forth across the country, and territorial newspapers published stories of returning prospectors. Mass-circulation newspapers that were hungry for articles to fill their columns eagerly reprinted news of strange discoveries from territorial newspapers. The time was ripe for adventurers to make their name by exploring the headwaters of the Yellowstone and Madison Rivers.

The area that became Yellowstone National Park was far too remote and rugged to attract permanent settlers to its mountain valleys, which were buried under deep snow for several months every year. But men began living on its edges in the 1860s. These settlers called their places "ranches," but they usually launched a variety of enterprises, such as farming, trapping, and fishing. Often, they became commercial hunters to meet the demand for elk hides after buffalo had been wiped out on the plains. The hides were needed to make leather belts for the country's growing number of mills and factories. Elk hunting took settlers deep into the wilderness.

Gilman Sawtell settled at Henrys Lake in what is now Idaho, about fifteen miles from the West Entrance of Yellowstone Park. He was a blue-eyed blond from Massachusetts who came west after the Civil War and staked his claim on the northeast edge of Henrys Lake.

Sawtell's main business was harvesting and selling fish from the five-hundred-acre lake, as many as forty thousand of them a year. He reportedly caught as many as 160 trout an hour, each averaging two and a half pounds, with a hook and line. In winter when the lake froze over, springs kept open a small area near Sawtell's compound. Fish swarmed the open water there, and Sawtell harvested them with a spear.

While launching his enterprises, Sawtell built a veritable village. He had several sturdy log buildings: a residence, a blacksmith shop, a stable, a storage shed for hides and game, and an icehouse. He apparently had guests in mind when he built the compound. His whitewashed house was big enough to accommodate twenty people and had numerous bedsteads, stools, and tables. He also kept enough stoneware to serve large groups.

In 1871, Sawtell guided a group of men from Virginia City and Deer Lodge, Montana, on a tour that covered the geyser basins, Yellowstone Lake, and the Grand Canyon of the Yellowstone. Because of this trip, Sawtell is credited with being the first commercial Yellowstone guide.

Another contender for that distinction was a rancher named Frederick Bottler, whom Philetus Norris, later Yellowstone Park's second superintendent, hired in 1870 to guide him through the park area. Their effort failed when Bottler fell into the snow-flooded Gardner River.

In 1867, the Fort Laramie Treaty forced the Crow Indians to cede their claims north and west of the Yellowstone River. That's when Fred Bottler decided to settle across the river from the reservation in the Paradise Valley, north of the park.

While Bottler was unloading his plow near the mouth of Trail Creek, he saw a group of Crow braves practicing maneuvers across the Yellowstone River. He put the plow back on his wagon and moved farther south to a spot across the valley from where miners worked their claims in Emigrant Gulch. The miners not only deterred the Indians but also provided a ready market for Bottler's produce.

Bottler staked his claim at a spot where cold springs bubbled out of the mountains and formed streams that provided water for irrigation. He plowed the land and soon had crops of hay, grain, and vegetables. He raised pigs, milked cows, and made butter in a churn turned by a small waterwheel.

Like Sawtell, Bottler didn't confine himself to agriculture. He was an innkeeper, a guide, and a commercial hunter. (Bottler sold more than two thousand elk hides in 1875.)[16] While prospecting in the 1860s, he explored the Upper Yellowstone, including the Firehole Basin.

His combination of skills made him an ideal candidate to join several early expeditions as a hunter and guide. In 1870, Bottler and Philetus Norris, who became the second park superintendent, climbed Electric Peak while scouting the area. Bottler also earned praise in the journals of several early explorers and adventurers, including F. V. Hayden, who led the first official government surveys of Yellowstone in 1871 and 1872, and an English nobleman, the Earl of Dunraven, in 1874. Dunraven described Bottler as "active, strong, willing and obliging, a keen hunter always in good humor, capable of enduring great hardships, and a capital hand at making a comfortable camp."[17]

After gold was discovered at Grasshopper Creek in southwest Montana in 1862, prospectors fanned out to scour every gully and creek within hundreds of miles. A survey expedition led by Walter Washington DeLacy was typical.

In 1863, DeLacy was elected leader of a group of about forty prospectors, which was large enough to rebuff Indian attacks.[18] In early August, this group assembled south of Virginia City, circled around the area that was to become Yellowstone Park, and headed up the Snake River. They camped periodically and spread out in small groups to look for gold. The men went up the South Snake River to its source, where they divided into two groups. Both groups crossed over the Continental Divide and eventually came to the Lower Geyser Basin. They didn't find gold in paying quantities, but they did bring back information about the wonders they had seen.

No doubt the prospectors told wild stories of towering geysers and crystal-clear boiling springs in the saloons and parlors of Montana gold camps. Some of these outlandish prospector stories filtered back to Eastern newspapers. On August 31, 1867, the *Montana Post* published an article about a group of prospectors who had been to the headwaters of the Yellowstone River. It reported:

Walter DeLacy led a group of gold prospectors into Wonderland in 1863. He published the first map of the area that showed prominent features accurately.

For eight days they traveled through a volcanic country emitting blue flame, living streams of molten brimstone, and almost every variety of minerals known to chemists. The appearance of the country was smooth and rolling, with a long level plain intervening. On the summits of the roiling mounds were craters for four to eight feet in diameter; and everywhere on the level plain, dotting it like prairie dog holes, were smaller ones, from four to six inches upwards. The stem and blaze was constantly discharging from these subterranean channels in regular evolutions or exhaustions, like the boilers of our steamboats and gave the same roaring, whistling sound. As far as the eye could trace, this motion was observed. They were fearful to ascent to the craters lest the thin crust should give way and swallow them.

An abbreviated version of the *Post*'s account circulated across the country for several weeks. The newspapers that published it included the *New York Times*, the *Chicago Tribune*, and the Honolulu *Pacific Commercial Advertiser*.

In 1865, DeLacy, who worked as a cartographer in the Montana Territory Surveyor General's Office, was asked to prepare an official "Map of the Territory of Montana with portions of the Adjoining Territories." His map showed Yellowstone Lake and Falls and a "hot spring valley" at the site of the Firehole geyser basins. But DeLacy didn't publish a narrative account of what he saw until 1876. By that time, credit for the discovery of Yellowstone Park had been claimed by members of the Washburn Expedition of 1870.

BEFORE THE WASHBURN EXPEDITION IN 1870, SEVERAL EFFORTS TO CONvene an exploration party had fizzled because organizers could not attract a large enough group to repel Indian attacks. But in 1869, three men, David E. Folsom, Charles Cook, and William Peterson, decided a small group could sneak by the Indians for a visit. The trio skirted the Crow Reservation by staying on the west side of the Yellowstone River. North of the boundary that would come to define the park, they encountered two elderly Sheepeater Indian women who were drying chokecherries for winter food. They were the only Indians they saw on their thirty-six-day trip. But they did see a long list of Yellowstone wonders, including Tower Fall, Lamar Valley, the Grand Canyon and Falls of the Yellowstone, Yellowstone Lake, and geysers at West Thumb, Shoshone Lake, and the Lower and Middle Geyser Basins.[19]

At first, Folsom and Cook were reluctant to write about what they had seen. As Folsom said later, "I doubted if any magazine editor would look upon a truthful description in any other light than the production of the too-vivid imagination of a typical Rocky Mountain liar.[20]"

At the behest of a friend who had connections to New York publishing, Folsom and Cook prepared a manuscript that merged the separate diaries they kept during the trip. When they submitted the manuscript for publication, Folsom discovered that his fears of rejection were well founded. The *New York Tribune, Scribener's*, and *Harper's* magazines all turned it down. The reason they gave was that they had reputations "they could not risk with such unreliable material."[21]

Finally, the men succeeded in getting the manuscript published in the less-prestigious Chicago-based *Western Monthly* in June 1870. By that time, plans were under way for the famous Washburn Expedition that would get publishers' attention.

When Philetus Norris heard that plans were under way to launch a Yellowstone exploration party leaving in August, he decided to get there first. In June—long before the snow melted off the Yellowstone High Country—Norris made his way from Bozeman to Fred Bottler's ranch in the Paradise Valley of the Yellowstone River, north of the park area. He stayed for several days and persuaded Fred Bottler to serve as his guide. The pair headed up the Yellowstone River while spring runoff was still high. Norris said rugged terrain, tangled fallen timber, and streams swollen by melting snow "made our progress—mainly on foot leading our horses—slow, tedious and dangerous, we persevered until near a large river."[22]

Although the Gardner River was only twenty feet wide and knee deep, Fred Bottler lost his footing while trying to cross it, and the raging torrent dragged him away. Norris ran downstream while the river bashed Bottler into boulders. Finally, Bottler grabbed an overhanging cottonwood branch and climbed out with Norris's help, but his rifle, ammunition, and hat had been swept away.

The men waited overnight while Bottler's elk skin garments dried. The next morning, Norris took his field glasses and scanned the area. In the distance, he could see clouds of steam rising from Mammoth Hot Springs. He was headed in the right direction, but without Bottler's rifle to harvest game and fend off Indians who might be in the area, the men decided they had to turn back.

David E. Folsom was part of a three-man group that toured the Yellowstone Park area in 1869. He had trouble finding a publisher for the account he co-wrote because they didn't believe him.
NATIONAL PARK SERVICE

Norris considered joining the Washburn Expedition but decided that there was "very little prospect of exploration that year."[23] He thought opportunities would be better with Northern Pacific Railroad survey parties on the Columbia River and went to join them.

When Norris returned to Montana several weeks later, he said he was "mortified" to hear the news that the Washburn Expedition had successfully explored the Upper Yellowstone and that his friend Truman Everts had barely survived thirty-seven days in the wilderness after wandering away from the group.

Had Norris succeeded, he probably would have been credited with being the "discoverer" of Yellowstone Park. He had the gravitas to have his reports taken seriously and the connections to get them published. Norris's effort to explore the park area made it clear that the race for exploration was on by the summer of 1870.

CHAPTER TWO

Recruiting Good Men

By the late 1860s, the evidence of wonders at the headwaters of the Yellowstone and Madison Rivers was overwhelming. An article in the June 8, 1867, issue of the Virginia City *Montana Post* said:

> *If the evidence of those avant gardes, the hunter and the prospector is admissible, and it is corroborative from a score of different persons going thither at different seasons, from different places by different routes, and without subsequent collusion, there exists on the extreme borders of the Territory and extending southward, a region of country surpassing in natural curiosities any other on the continent, and offering a most tempting field for scientific exploration, as well as the most enticing for tourists, artists, sensation hunters and miners, of any region lying within the confines of the Republic. A terra incognita, where description remains to be written, abounding and wonderful, the grand and golden. The stories related of it seem fabulous, but the testimony is cumulative and worthy of credence.*

The *Post* went on to describe "petrified forests," "a volcanic region covered with lava," and "an immense geyser that throws a huge column of water fifty feet." The area, the *Post* claimed, contains immense gravel bars "said to prospect richly in gold" and "water covered with a tar-like substance that suggest the presence of oil."

"A party is now forming, purposing in few weeks to visit this region, but a few days ride from Virginia [City] on a trip of exploration and pleasure. It will be sufficiently large to ensure safety from Indians and will consist of gentlemen fully competent to portray with pen and pencil the beauties, wonders and solid realities of this terrestrial arcana."

The expedition that the *Post* said would launch in the summer of 1867 never materialized, but the case the *Post* made for exploration must have been common knowledge. Nathaniel Pitt Langford probably read the *Montana Post* article.

When Langford set about organizing an expedition in the summer of 1870, he looked for men who met the criteria the report listed. The first thing he did was to arrange for an Army escort. Where the *Post* called for "gentlemen," Langford looked for prominent men (government officials and entrepreneurs) whose credibility couldn't be questioned, and for skilled writers with the connections to get their descriptions published. He wanted a large group of dignitaries and sought to have it accompanied by an Army escort to protect it from Indians.

Langford never said much about why he organized the Washburn Expedition, but apparently it wasn't solely for fame and adventure. On June 4 and 5, 1870, he and the financier Jay Cooke met in New York City. At that time, Cooke owned a controlling interest in the Northern Pacific Railroad. What took place at the meeting is unknown, but Langford ended his long stay in the East, returned to Montana, and began organizing an expedition. His conversation with Cooke must have motivated him.

On the way back, he stopped to visit members of his family in Saint Paul, and while there he met with Major General Winfield S. Hancock, who commanded the Military Department of Dakota, which included the Montana Territory. He apparently persuaded General Hancock to look favorably on an application for an Army escort for an exploration party.

Although Langford never claimed he was the organizer of the expedition, shortly after he got back to Montana he apparently began planning it. In his book, he wrote: "About the first of August 1870, our plans took definite shape, and some twenty men were enrolled as members of the exploring party."[1] He also said Crow Indians had been raiding in the Yellowstone and Gallatin Valleys. The Crow were peaceful at that time, so it is more likely that Sioux or Blackfeet were marauding in the area.

It's not known exactly how men came to join the exploration group. Langford has been called the "spark plug" behind the expedition, so he probably recruited most of the members.[2] After word spread that a serious expedition was being planned, others must have volunteered. Judging from the composition of the group, two criteria were paramount for membership. First, the men had to have sterling reputations so their reports of the things they saw could not be doubted. Second, at least some of them had to be skilled writers who had the contacts they needed to get their descriptions published.

Most of the explorers weren't experienced outdoorsmen, although Langford must have wanted such men. Among the men Langford mentioned was Montana pioneer James Stuart, who along with his brother, Granville, made the first recorded gold strike in the territory in 1858. In 1863, he led a party of fifteen prospectors from Bannack to the lower Yellowstone Valley. A hundred and fifty hostile Indians attacked them, killing three men and wounding others. To avoid another attack, Stuart led his men on a circuitous eighteen-hundred-mile route on the Oregon Trail back to Bannack.[3]

When Stuart heard that the exploration party Langford was putting together had dwindled to eight, he wrote a letter, saying, "That is not enough to stand guard, and I won't go into that country with out a guard every night" and the expeditions wouldn't be safe with fewer than fifteen men "and not very safe with that number."[4]

At the end of his letter, Stuart recanted and said, "I will take that back, for I am just damned fool enough to go anywhere anybody else is willing to go—only I want it understood that very likely some of us will lose our hair."[5] By the time the expedition finally departed, Stuart had been called for jury duty and couldn't go. Langford lamented the loss of Stuart because he was both a prominent citizen and an experienced outdoorsman who could have added credibility and knowledge to the expedition. He said, "In case we had trouble with Indians Stuart's services would be worth those of half a dozen men."[6]

In the late 1860s, several efforts were made to launch explorations, but they all fizzled, usually because of hostile Indians riled up by increased encroachment onto their traditional lands. By 1870, Indian troubles had settled down. In 1867, the US Army established Fort Ellis just east of Bozeman and troops from there began maintaining order in the area. Also, the Fort Laramie Treaty of 1868 defined the boundaries of the Crow Reservation, and that tribe mostly stayed peacefully east and south of the Yellowstone River. However, Sioux and Cheyenne continued to raid near the park area.

There was no doubt that the area provided an opportunity to gain fame and fortune. What was needed was the right person to seize the opportunity. Nathaniel Pitt Langford had just the right combination of characteristics to organize such an expedition. In 1868, the thirty-eight-year-old Langford resigned his position as commissioner of internal revenue for Montana Territory with the understanding that President Andrew Johnson would name him its governor. But the US Senate refused to confirm his appointment, so Langford was unemployed, and he had the time to promote an expedition.

By 1870, Langford had been in Montana Territory for six years. He had listened to prospectors returning from the park area and sought out aging trappers, including the famous Jim Bridger, for descriptions of what they had seen. That made him well versed in Yellowstone lore, and he could use his knowledge to persuade people to join the expedition. As territorial tax assessor, he knew all the prominent Montana citizens, so he could recruit them. Also, as the scion of an influential family, Langford had the connections he needed back east to get support from businessmen, politicians, and military officials. Most important, Langford was an ambitious man who sought to leave his mark on history.

Although Langford was the principal organizer of the expedition, General Henry Dana Washburn was chosen as its leader. It's unclear how this choice was made, but General Washburn certainly was a highly respected citizen with an excellent record as a leader.

Washburn was born in Vermont in 1832 but moved to Ohio with his parents that year. He went to school in Ohio until he was thirteen, when he was apprenticed to a tanner. He abandoned that trade and became a schoolteacher in Indiana. After preparatory work at Oberlin College, he got a law degree at New York State and National Law School. He opened a law office in Indiana in 1854 and married. The Washburns had four children before the Civil War.

At the beginning of the Civil War, in 1861, Washburn raised a company of volunteers in Indiana and the governor commissioned him a lieutenant colonel. He led his men in battles in the western and eastern fronts of the war. At the battle of Vicksburg, he caught wasting consumption disease, which weakened him for the rest of his life. He eventually achieved the rank of brevet major general.

While still in the Army, Washburn was pressed to run for US Congress from Indiana and served two terms, but he decided not to seek a third. He asked his old commander, President Ulysses Grant, to appoint him surveyor general of Montana in hopes that life in the West would improve his health, and he moved to the territory in 1869.

General Henry Dana Washburn was the surveyor general of Montana. He proved to be a most able leader of the expedition that bears his name.

He became interested in exploring the park area and used his connections to help secure the Army escort for the expedition. He proved to be an excellent leader who unified the diverse collection of men with strong personalities and made necessary plans and decisions, such as the posting of nightly guards. Despite his weakened health, he frequently rode ahead of the group to scout the route and took on guard duty when needed.

Cornelius Hedges, a graduate of Yale and Harvard Law School, was an important member of the Washburn Expedition. He was born in Massachusetts in 1831 and grew up there as part of a farming family. After he graduated from Yale in 1853, he taught school in Connecticut and "read law." After a year, he went to Harvard and got his law degree in 1855. Hedges married in 1856 and moved to Iowa, where he opened a law office in 1857. He also assisted as an editor at a local newspaper.

In 1864, Hedges moved his family back to Connecticut and struck out for the gold fields of Montana. He worked several claims in Virginia City, then headed to the new gold rush town of Helena, where he began a successful law practice and wrote for the *Helena Herald*.

N. P. Langford claimed that Hedges was the first to suggest that the area the Washburn Expedition visited be set aside as a national park. Langford said that occurred when the party was about to leave that area and camped where the Gibbon and Firehole Rivers run together to form the Madison. Historians doubt this campfire story, but it is clear that Hedges was a strong advocate for Yellowstone Park for the remainder of his life. Also, the idea of setting the area aside had been proposed at least twice before the Washburn Expedition even began. Acting territorial governor Thomas Francis Meagher proposed the idea as early as 1865, and David E. Folsom reiterated it when he returned from an 1869 visit there.

Hedges was an avid angler who never missed an opportunity to fish. and he stocked the Washburn Expedition larder when supplies were running low because of the delay caused by the search for the missing Truman C. Everts. Hedges also wrote a set of articles about the Washburn Expedition for the *Helena Herald*.[7]

Warren Gillette was the best outdoorsman of the Washburn Expedition. It was a reputation he earned by traveling to the Dakotas by steamboat, then crossing through Indian country on the Montana plains. He arrived in Montana early enough to follow gold rushes first to Deer Lodge, then Bannack, then to Virginia City, and finally to Helena. In addition to searching for gold,

Cornelius Hedges was a member of the Washburn Expedition. A prominent Montana attorney, he was a powerful advocate for establishing Yellowstone Park.

Gillette set up stores and became an important merchant. The thirty-eight-year-old Gillette was born in New York and attended Oberlin College. He worked in Ohio and Illinois in the fur business.

News of the Idaho gold rush in 1862 lured him to the West, but by the time he got to Montana, gold had been discovered there, so he turned to running businesses. Gillette joined a partner in his store in Virginia City, and they moved their merchandise to Helena after gold was discovered there in 1864. Their retail business led them into freighting from Fort Benton, the last port for steamboats up the Missouri River.

Gillette and his partner decided to build a toll road through an impassable canyon to shorten the trip. They did most of the hard physical work on the road themselves. The highly profitable road was finished in 1866.

Gillette's standing as a successful businessman and his outdoor experience gained as a prospector, freighter, and road builder made him an attractive candidate for the Washburn Expedition. All he lacked was a credential as a writer. Although Gillette kept a diary of the trip, he never published anything about it. The diary wasn't published until 1972.[8]

Gillette's most remarkable contribution to the expedition occurred when he insisted on staying behind the others to search for Everts with two soldiers from the Army escort. After four days, Gillette ended his futile search. In his diary entry for that day, he wrote, "Where is the poor man Everts—is he alive? is he dead? in the mountains wandering, he knows not whither? or back home safely? Did he kill his horse? if so I wonder how he likes Horseflesh? With dried horse meat he could live thirty or forty days. How he must have suffered even at the best! The reflection that he may be within ten or fifteen miles of us."

Like Warren Gillette, Samuel Thomas Hauser was lured to the West by news of the Idaho gold strike of 1862, and he came up the Missouri River by steamboat. After he landed in Fort Benton, Hauser made his way to Idaho, but he soon came back to the newer diggings at Bannack, Montana.

Hauser was born in 1833 in Kentucky and was educated in public schools there, supplemented by tutoring from a cousin who was a Yale graduate. In 1854, Hauser went to Missouri to be a surveyor for the Missouri Pacific Railroad. In less than ten years, he was the chief engineer on the Lexington branch of the Missouri Pacific.

Hauser was a member of the James Stuart party that searched the lower Yellowstone for gold in 1863. When Indians attacked the party, they shot

Samuel Thomas Hauser used his skills as a civil engineer to estimate the heights of waterfalls and geyser eruptions. He failed in his effort to measure the elevation of Grand Teton.

Hauser in the chest. Fortunately, he was carrying a thick notebook in a breast pocket that stopped the rifle ball just over his heart.

In 1865, N. P. Langford helped Hauser and a partner start a bank in Virginia City. Soon, Hauser had banking interests in nearly every city in Montana. He also built the first smelter in the territory.

While with the Washburn Expedition, Hauser used his surveying skills to estimate the heights of waterfalls and the eruptions of geysers. He also kept a diary of the trip.

President Abraham Lincoln appointed Truman C. Everts federal tax assessor for Montana Territory in 1864. That was a patronage job, and he lost it when Ulysses S. Grant became president. His former job made Everts a prominent Montana citizen, and he was available to join the Washburn Expedition.

The nearsighted Everts gained nationwide fame after he strayed away from the expedition and became lost and alone in the Yellowstone wilderness for thirty-seven days. Newspapers across the country reported his being lost and the miraculous story of his being found. He published a highly colored account of his adventure in the popular *Scribner's Monthly*, bringing attention to the effort to establish Yellowstone Park.

At fifty-four, Everts was the oldest member of the Washburn Expedition. He was born in Vermont in 1816, one of six boys in his family. His father was a Great Lakes ship captain, and Everts was his cabin boy on several voyages. Nothing more is known of his early life or education. His appointment as territorial tax assessor indicates that he was a staunch Republican.

Walter Trumbull had been Truman Everts's assistant, a position he probably owed to the fact that his father was US senator Lyman Trumbull of Ohio. Despite his father's influence, young Trumbull lost his job when Grant became president. At twenty-four, he was the youngest member of the expedition.

Trumbull was born in Springfield, Illinois, and attended public schools there. He attended the US Naval Academy but resigned his commission at the end of the Civil War. After that, he became a reporter for the *New York Sun*. In Montana, he was a contributor to the *Helena Rocky Mountain Gazette*, and he wrote an article about the expedition for the *Overland Monthly*.

Benjamin Stickney was the commissary for the Washburn Expedition and served a critical role managing their dwindling supplies when they extended their time to search for Everts.

Stickney was born in New York in 1838, and he worked on the family farm in Illinois until he was nineteen. He worked in railroad construction for a while, then moved to Colorado, where he began prospecting.

In 1863, he bought a team and wagon and hauled a load of provisions to sell in the booming gold camp at Virginia City, Montana. He used his profits to start freighting and mining businesses.

Jacob Ward Smith was a late addition to the Washburn Expedition, one whose antics aggravated its organizer and main chronicler, N. P. Langford. It's no surprise that the prim and proper Langford wouldn't like the boisterous Smith, who loved gambling at card games and practical jokes and who had an acerbic wit. Langford said of Smith: "He seemed to think that his good-natured non-sense would always be a passport to favor and be accepted in the stead of real service."[9]

Smith was born in New York City and learned to be a butcher working in his stepfather's street-market stall, which probably shaped his personality. That's also where he met his wife, the daughter of a fishmonger.

Jake Smith wasn't the wastrel Langford made him out to be. In 1861, Smith and his wife moved to Virginia City, Nevada, where he entered business and politics. He speculated in silver and accumulated a modest fortune as a stockbroker. He was also elected to Nevada's first legislature.

He moved to Montana in 1866 and went into the tanning business. That enterprise failed two years later, so Smith was available to join the Washburn Expedition in the summer of 1870.

N. P. Langford considered only the nine government officials and businessmen to be members of the expedition. He said of them: "I question if ever there was a body of men organized for an exploring expedition, more intelligent or more keening alive to the risks to be encountered than those enrolled."[10]

The expedition hired Elwood Bean and Charles Reynolds to manage the packhorses carrying their supplies. The expedition also had two cooks whose status as African Americans was such that they didn't warrant last names in accounts of the trip. The cooks were called Johnny and Nute.

Lieutenant Gustavas Cheney Doane commanded an Army escort of five men that accompanied the Washburn Expedition. The thirty-year-old Army officer was stationed at Fort Ellis, near Bozeman, Montana. He was born in Illinois in 1840, and he moved to Oregon with his parents as a child in 1846, then to the California gold camps in 1849. No doubt those frontier experiences contributed to his prowess as an outdoorsman.

After Doane graduated from the University of the Pacific, he joined the Army and moved through the enlisted ranks from private to sergeant and was commissioned a first lieutenant in 1864. He saw action around Washington, DC, and Vicksburg, Mississippi. He mustered out of the Army in 1866.

After the war, Doane helped set up a merchandising business in Yazoo City, Mississippi, where he married his first wife, Amelia Link, the daughter of a wealthy landowner. After he failed in business and at farming his father-in-law's land, he went to Illinois.

He rejoined the Army in 1868 as a second lieutenant. After assignments in Nebraska and Wyoming, he was assigned to Fort Ellis, near Bozeman, Montana. There, he promptly gained a reputation as an Indian fighter. He commanded one of four cavalry companies that attacked a band of Blackfeet Indians near the Marias River in northwest Montana on January 23, 1870. About two hundred Indians, mostly women and children, were killed in what came to be called The Marias Massacre. The Army had been sent to suppress a band that was accused of marauding and killing a white settler, but they attacked an innocent band.

The massacre prompted a series of Army inquiries that revealed conflicting reports that led to a change in federal policy toward Indians and appointment of Indian agents recommended by religious organizations. Doane's role in the battle and the subsequent reports were controversial, but he won praise as an Indian fighter in Montana.

As soon as Lieutenant Doane heard there was to be a Yellowstone expedition, he began lobbying to command its escort and was successful in his effort.

Doane's second in command was Sergeant William A. Baker, an Irishman who had enlisted in the Army in 1854 and earned his stripes during the Civil War. There were also three privates: Charles Moore, a Canadian who enlisted in 1868 and is remembered as the first person to draw pictures of Yellowstone features like the Lower Falls of the Yellowstone and the Grand Geysers; John Williamson from Maryland, who was chosen along with Private Moore to accompany Warren Gillette on his desperate search for Truman Everts when the tax collector became lost on the east shore of

In 1869 Charles W. Cook toured the area that became Yellowstone Park and co-wrote the first magazine article published about it.

Yellowstone Lake; and George McConnell, a farm boy from Indiana who served as Lieutenant Doane's orderly on the expedition.

It seems odd that not a single member of the Washburn Expedition had visited the park area before. Trappers, hunters, prospectors, and settlers had been visiting the area for decades, and many of them were living in Montana when the party was recruited.

By early August 1870, the membership of the expedition was established. It included nine prominent government officials and entrepreneurs, men whose solid reputations meant their descriptions of what they saw could not be doubted. Several of the men were accomplished writers who had connections to get their accounts published in a timely manner. Each man was to provide his own saddle horse and another horse for the pack train.

The group assembled in Bozeman on August 20, where they were feted as honored guests. The next day, they moved to a camp east of Fort Ellis after arrangements had been completed for their Army escort. At first, a full company of cavalry from Fort Ellis was supposed to accompany the expedition, but most of the men in the garrison had been deployed to keep peace with Indians. Only a lieutenant, a sergeant, and five enlisted men were assigned to the escort. They were supplied with abundant ammunition, forty days' rations, two extra saddle horses, and six pack mules.

The expedition departed for Wonderland on the afternoon of August 22.

John H. Baronett's familiarity with the area was so thorough that he was called "Yellowstone Jack." The forty-three-year-old Scotsman had already had a colorful career by 1870. He had gone to sea at an early age and deserted ship in 1850 to join the California gold rush. He also prospected for gold in Australia and Africa. Baronett fought for the Confederacy as a member of the First Texas Cavalry. More important, Baronett came to Montana in 1864 and joined a prospecting party that crossed the Yellowstone plateau. He also was with prospectors in the area in 1866 and 1869. No doubt Baronett was among the men most familiar with the park area in 1870. When the nearsighted tax assessor Truman Everts strayed away from the Washburn Expedition and was lost, Baronett and a companion went to the park area fully confident that they could find him.

Another obvious candidate for the expedition was Walter DeLacy, who had led a group of prospectors into the park area in 1863 and knew its features well. When Montana was made a territory in 1864, the legislature turned to DeLacy to prepare an official map. He included the area on his map, and it noted such features as a huge lake at the head of the Yellowstone River and a "hot spring valley" at the head of the Madison River. He continued to update his map and make corrections when travelers provided him new details. DeLacy was fifty-one years old in 1870, and had he joined the expedition, he would not have been its oldest member. DeLacy was surveying a railroad route in Idaho in the summer of 1870, but Washburn probably could have reassigned him.

David Folsom, who was just thirty-one, also worked in the surveyor general's office in 1870. Folsom, along with Charles W. Cook and William Peterson, had toured the park just a year before along the general route planned for the Washburn Expedition. Doubtless having someone along who had recently traveled the route would have been a great help. It's not known why Folsom wasn't on the expedition. Also, Folsom had collaborated with DeLacy to refine his "Map of the Territory of Montana and Adjoining Territories" so it included a more accurate description of the Yellowstone area. The 1870 edition of DeLacy's map came off the presses in time for the expedition to carry a copy on the trip.

In the spring of 1870, Philetus Norris hired Paradise Valley rancher Fred Bottler to guide him into the area that became Yellowstone National Park. Norris's effort ended after Bottler fell while crossing the Gardner River and lost his rifle at the edge of the park.

Bottler had hunted and prospected in the area many times, and he guided several groups of explorers and tourists into it over the years. He would have been an excellent addition to the Washburn Expedition. On the way to the park, the expedition stopped near Bottler's ranch in the Paradise Valley of the Yellowstone River, north of what became the park. Members of the expedition conferred with Bottler, but there's no mention of any effort to recruit him.

Gillman Sawtell was another rancher who had settled near the edge of what became the park and was available as a guide. Sawtell had settled at Henrys Lake in Idaho in the 1860s. No one knows exactly when Sawtell began visiting the area, but he was telling tales of fountains of boiling water in Virginia City by the mid-1860s. He was credited with being the park's first paid guide for escorting a party led by US commissioner of mines Rossiter Raymond in 1871, just one year after the Washburn Expedition.

It's clear that there were many men who had traveled the park area in the Montana Territory in 1870, but none of them went with the Washburn Expedition. Most were uneducated ranchers or prospectors, and they might have lacked the requisite prestige or writing skill to warrant an invitation. Perhaps Langford and other organizers of the Washburn Expedition just didn't want a guide. After all, it's hard to claim to have discovered something if a guide shows it to you.

CHAPTER THREE

Into the Wilderness

By the middle of August, plans had been completed for the long-talked-of expedition to the headwaters of the Yellowstone and Madison Rivers, a journey that would settle any questions about marvels there. Some members of the expedition met at 9:00 a.m. on August 17 with General Washburn at the surveyor general's office in Helena. From there, they would begin their hundred-mile trip to Bozeman to join an Army escort at Fort Ellis, a few miles east of the town. Others would join them along the way.

In the afternoon, a north wind blew in an unusual summer snowstorm, and several of the men stopped to spend the night at Half Way House, an inn between Helena and Bozeman. They had a good supper and played cards by a warm fire while the packers and cooks they had hired camped out in the snow.

Nathaniel Langford rushed ahead while the others waited out the storm. As grand master of the Montana Masonic Lodges, he had lodge business to attend to in Bozeman, and he wanted to confer with the commander at Fort Ellis about the Army escort for the expedition. He stopped at noon to eat in Radersburg, and the storm caught him when he approached Gallatin City, a town near where the Madison, Jefferson, and Gallatin Rivers ran together to form the Missouri. But he rushed on through the snow and arrived in Bozeman at about 7:00 p.m. on August 19.

On August 20, Langford met Major Eugene Baker, the commanding officer at Fort Ellis, to arrange the Army escort for the expedition. Baker said he couldn't provide one because all of his men were in the field fighting Indians, but Langford told Baker he had an order for one from the officer's superiors. Baker said the most he could spare was only a half dozen men, and Langford said that would be enough to maintain a good guard.

Langford later observed, "A small body of white men can more easily elude a band of Indians than can a large party, and without hesitating to consider the possible defense which we could make against a war party of hostile Sioux with this limited number, we declared ourselves satisfied, and took our departure for the terra incognita as fully assured of a successful journey as if our number had been multiplied by hundreds."[1]

The arrival of the rest of the party the next day caused quite a stir because it was rare for so many distinguished gentlemen to come to the tiny town all at once. Bozeman had a population of fewer than two hundred then. General Lester Willson, a prominent Bozeman merchant and trader, invited the visiting dignitaries to a formal supper with coffee, cake, and fruit, an honor they hadn't expected. In addition to Mrs. Willson, two eligible young ladies attended the event. That was a real treat; in territorial Montana, men still outnumbered women by a wide margin, and there were several bachelors in the group.

Cornelius Hedges was embarrassed to attend the gathering because he didn't have a white collar to wear. Warren Gillette described the guests as "pretty rough looking men to come into the presence of three fine ladies."[2] After supper, Mrs. Willson played for the guests on her piano, which was a rare treat when such instruments could come to Montana only by steamboat or ox train. Warren Gillette described Mrs. Willson as "a genuine Yankee Girl, who can cook well, sing well, play well and turn her hand to anything that will make a home pleasant."[3]

After supper and cigars, the explorers returned to Bozeman's finest hotel, the Guy House, where they joined officers from Fort Ellis who were smoking cigars, drinking champagne, and listening to music provided by a banjo and guitar duo. It would be the last time the men slept in a bed for a month. Even so, Warren Gillette complained that his bed was hard and that his companion, Walter Trumbull, "was a miserable bedfellow."[4]

The next morning, the explorers had breakfast at the hotel then rushed around saying goodbye to their friends. In the afternoon, they set up camp about half a mile from Fort Ellis near the East Gallatin River and prepared supper there. Lieutenant Doane brought a large pavilion tent from the fort that provided shelter from the sun, wind, and cold that day—and throughout the exploration.

In the evening, Cornelius Hedges read the latest newspapers to the company. Ladies and gentlemen came to the camp to visit the travelers, and several prospectors who had been to the park area came to tell the group what

Jacob Ward Smith was an entrepreneur who went on the Washburn Expedition. He was jocular and had a barbed wit he used to puncture the pompous, which earned him the scorn of N. P. Langford.

to expect. Knowing the explorers would soon see the sights, the prospectors probably avoided exaggerated descriptions of canyons that plunged a mile deep or geysers that threw boiling water a thousand feet in the air. But even realistic descriptions would have been enticing.

Always eager to gamble at cards, businessman Jake Smith started a game of Twenty-One. He took a pint of dried beans from the party's supplies to be used as chips and doled them to each player for a dollar each. To entice the gamblers, he began crying out "No limit, gentlemen."

The game ended because Sam Hauser had to drive the carriage for one of the ladies who had been visiting the camp. When Hauser tried to cash in his winnings, his chips were worth more than the money Smith had collected, apparently because someone added extra beans to the pot. As Warren Gillette described it, Smith's "unlimited game came to an inglorious end."[5]

On the morning of August 22, the party got ready to leave the camp near Fort Ellis. Each man had brought a horse to ride and a packhorse to contribute to the supply train. The first order of business was to load the packhorses. That was an arduous task, because the animals weren't used to the bulky saddles.

Langford said, "There are but few of our party who are adepts in the art of packing, for verily it is an art acquired by long practice, and we look with admiration upon our packers as they 'throw the rope' with such precision, and with great skill and rapidity tighten the cinch and gird the load securely upon the back of the broncho."[6]

Although the expedition had hired experienced packers, it was eleven o'clock before the men had subdued the packhorses and loaded them. Then the men of the expedition mounted their horses and headed east toward the mountains. The party of nineteen followed by the pack train must have made a formidable sight. About six miles east of Fort Ellis, the party crossed the divide between the Gallatin and Yellowstone watersheds, where there was a striking view.

Lieutenant Doane said, "The summit affords a fine view of the beautiful Gallatin Valley, with its cordon of snow-capped peaks, its finely timbered water-courses, and its long grassy declivities, dotted with the habitations of pioneers, and blooming with the fruits of industry now ready for harvest."[7]

Langford also commented on the view of the valley the party was leaving. "The scene from this point is excelled in grandeur only by extent and variety. An amphitheater of mountains two hundred miles in circumference, enclosing a valley nearly as large as the state of Rhode Island, with all its details of pinnacle, peak, dome, rock and river, is comprehended at a glance."[8] He said the men could see all the way to where the Madison, Jefferson, and Gallatin Rivers ran together to form the Missouri, some thirty miles to the west.

On the evening of August 22, the party was camped away from civilization for the first time, so General Washburn established a guard routine. He wanted two men on duty at a time, with one shift from dusk to 1:00 a.m. and the other from 1:00 a.m. to dawn. Fourteen men were available for duty, which meant each man would serve two nights a week. Cooks and packers were excused from guard duty.

The guards weren't just to watch for Indians who might dare to attack the group or, more likely, to try to steal horses. They were also supposed to keep the horses from wandering away and to protect them from predators. Keeping mountain lions away from the horses would become crucial when the expedition went deeper into the wilderness.

Langford, ever fearful of Indians, said, "Fresh Indian signs indicate that the red-skins are lurking near us, and justify the apprehensions expressed in the letter which Hauser and I received from James Stuart, that we will be attacked by the Crow Indians. I am not entirely free from anxiety. Our safety will depend upon our vigilance."[9]

Others in the party did not share Langford's fear of the Crow, who had made peace with whites. In fact, the Crow frequently provided scouts to the Army in Indian wars against the Sioux, Cheyenne, and Nez Perce.

But Langford remained fearful and didn't like to be disagreed with. He said, "Jake Smith has sent the first demoralizing shot into the camp by announcing that he doesn't think there is any necessity for standing guard."[10] Langford went so far as to question the wisdom of letting Smith join the party. "One careless man," Langford said, "no less than one who is easily discouraged by difficulties, will frequently demoralize an entire company."[11] He added that saying he did not dread Indians when he saw a large force of them "would be a braggart boast."

The explorers continued down Trail Creek toward the Yellowstone River on August 23. When they reached the hills overlooking what is now called Paradise Valley, they could see a vista running thirty miles up and down the river. The volcanic mountains on the east side of the valley carved a jagged line across the blue sky where the tallest peaks reached nearly eleven thousand feet and were still capped with snow. Timber covered the sides of the mountains, and grass carpeted the wide valley floor.

In the afternoon, the explorers saw their first Indians. Langford said they came from the east side of the valley to the edge of a plateau overlooking the river and "conspicuously displayed themselves for a time to engage our attention."

Langford took this display as a warning. He said, "This early admonition of our exposure to hostile attack, and liability to be robbed of everything, and compelled on foot and without provisions to retrace our steps, has been the subject of discussion in our camp tonight, and has renewed in our party the determination to abate nothing of our vigilance, and keep in a condition of constant preparation."[12]

Two men who were behind the main group hunting for antelope said they saw at least a hundred Indians watching the pack train. When the Indians saw the pair, they turned their horses and disappeared behind a bluff.

Lieutenant Doane, an experienced Indian fighter, wasn't concerned. In his journal, he wrote simply, "This afternoon we met several Indians belonging to the Crow Agency."[13] Warren Gillette was even more dismissive, noting in his journal that he "saw three Crow Indians on the other side of the river. They did not come over to see us."[14] The Yellowstone River was the border of the Crow Reservation at that time, so Indians on the east side were on their own land and had made peace with whites.

That evening, the explorers arrived at the ranch belonging to Fred Bottler, who told them that twenty-five lodges of Crow Indians were traveling farther up the valley. The explorers camped near the ranch at the base of the foothills by a group of abundant springs that fed a small grove. Several men went fishing, using grasshoppers for bait in the Yellowstone River and catching several large fish.

Lieutenant Doane noted, "One may fish with the finest tackle of the eastern sportsman, when the water appears to be alive with them, all day long without a bite."[15]

Ever the avid angler, Hedges bragged that he caught the first fish that evening. He was usually the first to wet his line whenever the party camped near a stream.

That evening, Jake Smith conjured a challenge to replenish his supply of gambling money. He had lost his stake playing Twenty-One at Fort Ellis.

Each man in the expedition carried a revolver, ostensibly to protect himself against Indian attack. Smith said he doubted that any member of the party, except the expert marksman Sam Hauser, could hit an Indian with a revolver even at close range. As if to prove his point, Smith offered his hat as a target. He charged twenty-five cents a shot for the men to shoot at it from a distance of twenty yards.

Several men took up the challenge and blazed away at the hat with no success. They may not have been trying very hard, because they wanted to help the jovial Smith raise money to rejoin their card games.

But N. P. Langford apparently took the game seriously. He said, "I could not resist the inclination to quietly drop out of sight behind a clump of bushes, where from my place of concealment, I sent from my breech-loading Ballard repeating rifle four bullets in rapid succession, through the hat, badly riddling it."[16]

According to Langford, Smith asked, "Whose revolver is it that makes that loud report?"[17] Apparently, Smith didn't know about the ruse. He picked up his hat and said members of the group were better shots than he had expected.

Langford considered confessing his part in ruining Smith's hat and said he wished he had brought an extra to give the aggrieved man. Langford added, "I now wish that I had brought with me an extra hat. My own is not large enough for Jake's head. Notwithstanding the serious problems which we must deal with in making this journey, it is well to have a little amusement while we may."[18]

Smith immediately started another game of Twenty-One with his new stake. Warren Gillette said, "Fortune however favored him not, for he soon arose from his blanket without a cent; he stood his loss and the jest of the party with the greatest good humor."[19] But for the rest of the trip, Smith was always ready to gamble at cards and always seemed to have money to do it.

It rained overnight in the Paradise Valley, and the men awoke on August 24 to see fresh snow on the tall mountains across the river. Clouds clung to the mountainsides, but their base was visible so the explorers had a good view of the gold camp in Emigrant Gulch, across the valley.

Although it rained all morning, the sun came out by noon. By 2:30, the travelers' camp equipment had dried enough to pack, and the explorers moved on. After traveling six miles, the men made their way around a spur of the mountain and down a steep bluff.

There, the beautiful valley opened wide again. The east side of the valley was hemmed in by high lava mountains covered with stunted timber. Streams ran down from the mountains on the west side of the valley, where the explorers traveled. Cottonwood and chokecherry trees rose from the banks of the creeks. Grizzly bears had mangled the cherry trees for fruit. Waist-deep grass covered much of the valley floor.

After another six miles, the explorers came to the mouth of what is now called Yankee Jim Canyon and camped. Their mess table was well supplied with fish that anglers had caught in the morning and antelope, hare, ducks, and grouse that hunters had bagged during the day. That night, stars shone brightly through a clear sky. A chilly wind blew out of the canyon.

It was 40 degrees when the men got up on the morning of August 25. They packed their horses and threaded their way past enormous granite boulders that marked the entrance to Yankee Jim Canyon. They found a narrow trail where only one animal could pass at a time and crossed a spur of the mountain that overlooked the canyon where the river below them surged through the narrow canyon over huge boulders. Rattlesnakes hid in the crevices between broken rocks and shook their tails to announce their irritation at being disturbed.

The travelers scrambled over the rocks for two miles and came to a valley three miles wide. The land formation there was mostly limestone, where sagebrush covered the infertile soil of the valley floor. The explorers left the valley and crossed a succession of plateaus covered with sterile soil and marked with outcroppings of limestone.

After traveling twelve miles, the explorers came to the mouth of the Gardner River, which flowed into the Yellowstone River. They decided to wait to cross the rushing river and camped there although it was a poor sagebrush-covered spot with little grass. The explorers usually looked for ample grazing for the horses because they needed the animals to stay strong for the long journey. The men found petrified wood nearby and saw smoke from several fires in the mountains that indicated Indians were camped nearby, probably the twenty-five Crow lodges that Fred Bottler had told them about.

On the morning of August 26, Lieutenant Doane, along with Truman Everts and Private John Williamson, started ahead of the others in search of the best trail. The trio rode their horses across the Gardner River and turned eastward along the general course of the Yellowstone River. Certainly, heading up the Yellowstone was a sensible way to find the Grand Canyon and Falls, but this route took them away from Mammoth Hot Springs, which were only a few miles away.

Soon they found the mouth of the Yellowstone Canyon. The men decided the trail up the canyon was impassable, so they turned away from it toward the mountains. After crossing several ridges, they came to a rolling plateau dotted with groves of aspen and pine that extended as far as they could see. They soon came to the lower end of the Grand Canyon of the Yellowstone River.

Lieutenant Doane described the sight from the edge of the canyon: "Numerous falls are seen tumbling down from lofty summits a mere ribbon of in the immeasurable distance below. Standing on the brink of the chasm the heavy roar of the river comes to the ear only in a sort of hollow, hungry growl."

"Lofty pines on the bank of the stream dwindle to shrubs in the distance," Doane continued. "Numerous fish hawks are seen busily plying their vocation, sailing high above the waters, yet a thousand feet below the spectator. In the cliffs on the rocks down, hundreds of feet down, bald eagles have their eyries from which we can see them swooping still further into the depths to rob the ospreys of their hard earned trout."[20]

Doane left the canyon that he called "this empire of shadows and of turmoil" and led his men into a freshly burned plateau where fires that were probably set by Indians still smoldered.

On the way to the top of the plateau, Private Williamson killed an antelope, which they left for their companions who were following. The trio crossed high, rolling prairie for several miles and found tracks left by the unshod horses of Indians. They also found an abandoned colt, so they were sure Indians were not far ahead, but they went on unconcerned.

The trio continued across the plain that had been created by ancient lava flows. They passed a place where the lava had buckled and granite shafts protruded through. Doane said in wooded areas "they resemble dark icebergs stranded in an ocean of green, rising above the tops of the trees."[21]

Doane and his companions descended a deep ravine into a swampy valley and came to a spring the temperature of warm milk. They continued past the sulfur-laden spring on a trail that crossed a ridge and led down another deep ravine. They passed a small lake and found the remains of a recent Crow camp. The Indians that the trio followed had crossed the Gardner River and were headed away from the explorers. Doane's trio crossed Warm Spring Creek and found a campsite where they waited for the rest of the expedition.

After Doane and his companions left to search for a trail, the rest of the expedition prepared to move. By eleven o'clock, they were packed and began crossing the Gardner River, a rushing torrent twenty yards wide and three feet deep. Some of the packhorses floundered in the torrent and had to be repacked, which delayed travel. It was the same spot where Fred Bottler had fallen in the river just weeks before, causing Philetus Norris to abandon his exploration attempt. Just weeks earlier at this same crossing, Fred Bottler had fallen into the river.

Langford and his companions crossed over several rocky ridges protruding from the mountains toward the Yellowstone Canyon and came to what Langford called "The Valley of Desolation." They took a trail that led to the mouth of the canyon and, like Doane's scouting party, decided they couldn't get through and turned back and retraced their route for a quarter-mile.

They cut through the sagebrush and followed another trail up a steep, dry coulee. At the head of the coulee, they went through a tangle of fallen timber over a burnt and rocky road. The rough route jostled packsaddles loose, so the men had to stop to tighten them, making travel very slow. They also found the antelope carcass that Doane's scouting party had left for them and had to tie it to a packhorse, delaying travel even more.

By 3:00 p.m., their usual stopping time, the men had gone only six miles. They made just one move a day so they would have to pack their horses only once. They made camp in a pretty meadow by a cool stream they called "Antelope Creek."

As usual, Hedges rushed out to try the fishing, but he didn't catch anything. He spent the evening cleaning his pistol and mending his pants while the others played Twenty-One, except for Jake Smith, who was on guard duty.

The only tracks they had seen all day were from unshod Indian ponies, so Langford concluded that Doane and his companions had followed some other route. In his book, Langford said he noticed there were no trail marks from tepee poles, which indicated they were following Indian men on horseback who had sent their families by a gentler but more circuitous route. In his account in *Scribner's Monthly*, he contradicted that, saying simply that marks left by travois poles indicated Indians were nearby.

Langford was worried because the party was separated into two groups. "If we had been attacked," he wrote "our pack-train, horses, and stores would have been an easy conquest."[22]

Langford wrote, "Fortunately we were unmolested, and, when again united, made a fresh resolution to travel as much in company as possible." But he added that the resolve was soon neglected and "a day had scarcely passed when we were as reckless as ever." Apparently, other members of the expedition didn't share Langford's fear of these Indians, who must have been the peaceful Crow that Fred Bottler had told them about.

After setting up camp, Langford, Stickney, and Gillette scouted the area looking for a better route along the banks of the Yellowstone, but the effort failed. Langford and Hauser found tracks left by Doane and his companions and followed them to the brow of a mountain. They fired their guns to signal the scouting party and scanned the area with field glasses for an hour. But they saw no sign of campfires or grazing horses and returned to camp.

In the evening, Langford and Hedges decided to write in their journals. Langford said he sat on a sack of beans and Hedges on a sack of flour near where the other men were playing cards. Hedges said the game was poker. Langford doubted that "Deacon Hedges is sufficiently posted in the game to know,"[23] but he listened to the other man's explanation. Langford's description of what he saw reveals his priggery and ignorance of the game.

Langford wrote, "These infatuated players have put a valuation of five cents per bean, on beans that did not cost more than a dollar a quart in Helena."[24] Apparently, he did not understand that the beans were being used as tokens. He also accused Jake Smith of "a marvelous lack of veneration for his kinswoman" because he refers to beans as "his auntie." Of course Smith was saying "ante," which is a bet put in the pot before cards are dealt.

Langford seemed to understand the notion of beans as tokens when he noted that "Walter Trumbull has been styled the 'Banker,' and he says that at the commencement of the game he sold forty of these beans to each of the players, himself included (two-hundred in all), at five cents each."[25]

Problems arose when Smith insisted that Trumbull redeem his half-pint cup filled with beans. Trumbull explained that he had already redeemed two hundred beans.

"Reflecting upon their disagreement" Langford said, "I recall that about an hour ago Jake, with an apologetic 'Excuse me!' disturbed me while I was writing and untied the bean sack on which I am now sitting, and took from it a double handful of beans."[26]

Langford, who never missed an opportunity to belittle Smith, wrote, "It seems to me that a game of cards which admits of such latitude as this, with a practically unlimited draft upon outside resources, is hardly fair to all parties, and especially to 'The Banker.'"[27] Other members of the expedition don't mention the incident, and Smith didn't have difficulty starting card games later.

The similarity of the story of this game with dried beans as tokens and the one that happened at Fort Ellis days before raises questions. Perhaps Langford conflated the earlier story with an incident at this camp.

While Doane and his companions waited for the others to arrive on August 27, they explored the area around their camp. Doane assessed the geology of the area and noted the miners had dug several prospect holes there. But the major find of the day was the 115-foot fall of Warm Springs Creek that had cut its way through the rock of the canyon wall and left tall spires all around it. Doane described them thus: "Worn in every conceivable shape, these are very friable, crumbling under the slightest pressure; several of them stand like sentinels at the very brink of the fall."[28] The creek ran past these spires and plunged straight down in a single drop, and that's why its name is always singular, Tower Fall.

Meanwhile, Langford and his companions climbed to the summit of the divide that separated Antelope Creek from Tower Creek, then went down a steep canyon to the Yellowstone River. This, Langford said, was "where the wonders were supposed to commence."[29]

Indeed, wonders were starting to appear, just as people had said they would. Soon, in a small opening on the hillside, the men found three boiling springs that were not like anything they had seen before.

Cornelius Hedges described one of them as "an oval-shaped basin, twenty by forty feet in diameter. Its greenish-yellow water was hot, and bubbles of

Tower Fall was the first major sight seen by the Washburn Expedition. The men spent two days measuring the fall, climbing nearby spires, and exploring the area.

NATIONAL PARK SERVICE, PHOTO BY WILLIAM HENRY JACKSON, 1871

steam or gas were constantly rising from various parts of its surface." Another spring, he said, threw water "higher than our heads, and fearful volumes of stifling, sulfureous vapors were constantly escaping. The water was of a dark-lead color, and intensely hot."[30] The third spring was a thin boiling mush "in constant, noisy ebullition, emitting fumes of villainous smell."

They left the springs, climbed a ridge, and looked across the Yellowstone River. Langford said the east bank was composed of successive pillars of basalt standing thirty feet high and three to five feet in diameter. This "grand and impressive scenery," Langford said, "excited our attention until the gathering shades of evening reminded us of the necessity of selecting a suitable camp."[31]

The party descended to the bank of Tower Creek and camped about a mile from the Yellowstone River.

Hedges hiked down to the river to fish and caught four that weighed two and a half pounds each, but he ran out of grasshopper bait and returned to camp. The pack train, which usually lagged behind the others, arrived at about 4:00 p.m., and hunters, who had gone ahead to look for game, returned with a young deer. Hedges said he never tasted anything better than that fresh venison roasted over the campfire.

CHAPTER FOUR

Falls and Canyons

August 28 was a Sunday, so the men decided to take a day of rest. They were camped in a pleasant spot near a creek in an area that provided shade, grazing for the horses, and abundant fish and game. The place was so pleasant that Truman Everts called it "Camp Comfort." The name stuck.

Two hundred yards away, the creek plunged straight down the face of a cliff. As the creek approached the precipice, it passed between tall rock spires. Langford said, "Many of these are of faultless symmetry, resembling the minaret of a mosque; others are so grotesque as to provoke merriment as well as wonder."[1]

One of them was a rock fifty feet tall that the men named "The Devil's Foot" because of its hoof shape. It was the first time the travelers evoked images of the devil or hell in naming features that had bizarre shapes, sulfur smell, or intense heat. Many early travelers did that, but the park service has renamed most of them.

The explorers' first order of business was to measure the height of the fall. The civil engineer and surveyor, Sam Hauser, used trigonometry to estimate the fall at 110 feet. Benjamin Stickney was more direct. He climbed to the verge of the fall and dropped a rock tied to a strong cord to the bottom. Measuring the cord gave Stickney an estimate of 105 feet.[2]

Lieutenant Doane described what he saw when he climbed to the top of one of the formations: "A view from the summit of one of these spires is exceedingly beautiful; the clear icy stream plunges from a brink one hundred feet beneath to the bottom of the chasm, over two-hundred feet below, and thence rushes through the narrow gorge, tumbling over boulders and tree trunks fallen in the channel. The sides of the chasm are worn away into caverns lined with variously-tinted mosses, nourished by clouds of spray which rise from the cataract; while above, and to the left, a spur from the great plateau rises above all, with a perpendicular front of four-hundred feet."[3]

The Washburn Expedition spent three days measuring and exploring the Grand Canyon and Great Falls of the Yellowstone. Members of the party hiked to the bottom of the canyon.

When they began the expedition, members of the party agreed not to name any sights they saw after anybody in the party or any of their relatives and friends. The agreement caused a good-natured debate about the naming of the creek and fall. Walter Trumbull suggested "Minaret," and Sam Hauser suggested "Tower." The explorers debated the proposals, then voted for "Minaret" by a small margin.

The next evening, Hauser solemnly announced that the group had violated its agreement not to name features after people they knew. He claimed a well-known family, the Rhetts, lived in Saint Louis and had a "charming daughter" named Minnie. Hauser accused Trumbull of proposing her name, "Minnie Rhett," to honor his girlfriend. Trumbull denied Hauser's accusation, but Hauser insisted it was true. The men again put the question to a vote, and "Tower" won by a large majority. Later, it was surmised that it was Hauser who had a sweetheart in Saint Louis, a Miss Tower. Langford refused to take sides in the ongoing debate, but he said Trumbull always insisted that Hauser had cheated.

The only animal member of the expedition other than the horses was a large black dog named "Booby" that belonged to Nute, one of the African-American cooks. Booby was footsore after a week of running over rocky trails, so Nute made moccasins for him. At first, Booby tried to shake off the foot covers, but he soon got used to them and was again running around as the explorers traveled. Despite his name, Booby later proved to be a valuable member of the expedition by guarding the camp and guiding lost members home.

Lieutenant Doane said he spent the night of August 28 pacing back and forth in front of the campfire with a wet bandage wrapped around his arm to keep down pain from a felon, an injury that causes extreme pain at the fingertip. Doane described the pain in his infected right thumb as "absolute torture" and said he had lanced the felon three times with a dull pocketknife. Langford said he had offered to open the sore, but the young officer was "unwilling to submit to a thorough operation."[4]

General Washburn spent the day searching for a route to the wonders farther south while his men explored the area around Tower Fall. He came back to the camp at about three in the afternoon and reported seeing Yellowstone Lake from the top of a mountain. He told his companions he saw the Wind River Mountain Range to the east, and in the far distance to the south rose the jagged peaks of the Tetons.

The general's reconnaissance was a relief to the men who had wondered how they would make their way over the mountains ahead. Washburn had taken compass measurements to guide them past deep ravines and through the thick timber that could make it impossible to see landmarks.

Washburn's reports whetted the men's appetite for moving on. They had finally seen a boiling spring and a towering waterfall, and the general's report promised even more wonders ahead.

THE MORNING OF AUGUST 29 WAS SO COLD THAT A LAYER OF ICE FROZE ON the water buckets, but the men were up early and on their way by eight o'clock. The explorers headed south up the deep grade beside Tower Creek and began crossing country filled with creekbeds that ran parallel to the Yellowstone River. By following a ridge between two of these creeks eastward, they came to the first view of the Grand Canyon of the Yellowstone for most of the men.

Lieutenant Doane described the view "breaking through the lofty mountain ranges directly in front. Its perpendicular sides, wherever visible, of the yellow sulfuric tint above described, and its crest on either side of the river, mantled with heavy timber, extending beyond in an unbroken forest as far as the eye could reach."[5] The expedition was at the lower end of the canyon, about twenty miles north of where it begins.

Looking through the gap of the canyon, the men saw a vapor column rising several hundred feet. At first, they thought it must be smoke from a forest fire, but Lieutenant Doane said, "Someone noticed that the vapor rose in regular puffs, and as if expelled with a great force. Then the conviction was forced upon us. It was indeed a great column of steam, puffing away on the lofty mountainside, escaping with a roaring sound, audible at a long distance even through the heavy forest."[6]

Seeing bellowing steam made the men certain that they were approaching Wonderland, where they would see things the likes of which they had never seen before. Lieutenant Doane said "a hearty cheer rang out with the discovery."[7]

Buoyed by the sight, the party followed a ridge to the base of a large mountain. While the pack train continued around, others climbed to its summit, which was above the tree line, and the way was strewn with rocks.

Warren Gillette said from the top of the mountain "a beautiful view was spread upon all sides of us. To the east of south lay the Yellowstone Lake with its islands and promontories in plain sight, and flowing to the north came the Yellowstone River from the lake with silvery brightness and on either side dense black forests of spruce and pine seemed to hold it like a solid army of approaching men."[8]

The Grand Canyon of the Yellowstone was also in plain sight from the top of the mountain. Lieutenant Doane said, "Close beneath our feet, yawns the immense gulf of the Grand Canyon, cutting away the bases of two mountains in forcing a passage through the range. Its yellow walls divide the landscape nearly in a straight line to the junction of Warm Spring Creek below. The ragged edges of the chasm are from two hundred to five hundred yards apart, its depth so profound that the river bed is nowhere visible. No sound reaches the ear from the bottom of the abyss; the sun's rays are reflected on the further wall and then lost in the darkness below."[9]

Looking southward, Doane could see the three majestic peaks of the Tetons, Yellowstone Lake, and dozens of steam jets. He used his aneroid barometer to estimate the elevation of the mountain where he was standing at 9,966 feet.[10]

The explorers named the peak "Mount Washburn," after their leader who had climbed it the day before on his reconnaissance trip. This violation of their rule to not name sights after any member of the expedition set precedent. Several mountains were named for members of the expedition before the trip was over.

Doane and his companions headed down the mountain through pine forests filled with tracks from elk and mountain sheep along with bear scat. Doane shot at an elk, but it got away, and Jake Smith scared a young bear. They soon arrived at the camp set up by their packers and cooks, who had gone ahead. It was near a creek that ran into the Grand Canyon.

Following the creek by the camp downstream a mile, the men found an immense bed of volcanic ash. It was thirty feet deep and extended a hundred yards on both sides of the creek. A mile beyond the ash bed, they came to what Langford described as "a hideous-looking glen filled with sulfurous vapor emitted from five or six springs."[11] The entire surface of the area was covered with encrusted sinter, and jets of hot sulfur-stinking vapor shot up from hundreds of fissures and vents. One man thought it was like the entrance to hell. "It looked like nothing earthly we had ever seen,"[12] Langford said. The pungent fumes, he said, provided a "disagreeable sense of possible suffocation."

According to Langford, the springs were "all in a state of violent ebulli-tion, throwing their liquid contents up to three or four feet."[13] Occasionally, a spring threw up a cloud of steam rushing upward one hundred feet. The larg-est of the springs was about forty feet in diameter. Its greenish-yellow water was covered with bursting bubbles that stank of sulfur dioxide. One of the springs had a little chimney like a miner's cabin that emitted a steady stream of gas. Another chugged like a steam engine.

Nearby, a spring was filled with lead-colored bubbling mud the consis-tency of paint. The men shoved a stick into it that came back covered with slime a quarter of an inch thick. One of the men discovered a place where he could stand above a spring and shove a pole into it. The longest pole he could find never touched bottom.

The crust that surrounded the springs bent under a man's weight, and sulfur slime oozed out of the resulting cracks. One man risked his life to collect samples from the edge of a spring by lying down to spread his weight as widely as possible. He then rolled over to the edge of the spring, with the crust bending and sinking under him, grabbed a sample, and rolled back to safety.

Langford said the springs were so revolting that none of the men visited them twice. He observed, "The name of Hell Broth Springs, which we gave them, fully expressed our appreciation of their character."[14]

While their companions returned to camp, Lieutenant Doane, General Washburn, and Cornelius Hedges left Hell Broth Springs and continued exploring down the creek. After three miles, they came to a grove of dense timber on the brink of the Grand Canyon. The stream had carved a sheer wall fifteen hundred feet deep that ran into Grand Canyon of the Yellowstone. The men looked down into the abyss but couldn't see or hear the waters that rushed and tumbled over boulders thousands of feet below. The trio then returned to camp after sunset. Their sightseeing tour had taken them on a ten-mile walk.

The explorers left their camp near Hell Broth Springs at nine o'clock on the morning of August 30. They thought it would take them two or three days to reach the Falls of the Yellowstone, one of the wonders they had heard so much about. They knew they were at last in Wonderland.

Travel was slow because the men had to cross mountain ridges that ran toward the river and around patches of fallen timber. But as the noon hour approached, Langford said, the explorers were "greatly surprised to find ourselves descending the mountain along the banks of a beautiful stream in the immediate vicinity of the Great Falls of the Yellowstone."[15]

The explorers camped by a stream they dubbed "Cascade Creek" about a mile from the Lower Falls of the Yellowstone. The crystal-clear waters of the creek rushed through thick timber toward the Grand Canyon. About a quarter of a mile from the canyon, General Washburn said, the stream "tore its way through a mountain range making a fearful chasm through lava rock, leaving it in every conceivable shape." Doane said the gorge was filled with volcanic specimens: quartz, feldspar, mica, "in fact, everything from asbestos to obsidian."

The gorge was christened the "Devil's Den." Washburn said: "Below this is a beautiful cascade, the first fall of which is five feet, the second twenty feet, and the final leap eighty-four feet. From its exceedingly clear and sparkling beauty it was named Crystal Cascade."[16]

Apparently the explorers didn't reach the end of the cascade, where the creek plunges 129 feet to the bottom of the canyon between the Upper and Lower Falls. Their accounts don't mention Crystal Falls.

Langford worked by candlelight late into the night to record the day's events when Jake Smith called on him to "turn in." Langford couldn't resist using the remark as an excuse to criticize Smith: "Jacob is indolent and fond of slumber, and I think that he resents my remark to him the other day, that he could burn more and gather less wood than any man I ever camped with. He has dubbed me 'The Yellowstone Sharp.' Good! I am not ashamed to have the title."[17]

Langford decided to work until his candle burned out, writing, "There is in what I have already seen so much of novelty to fill the mind and burden the memory, that unless I write down in detail the events of each day, and indeed almost of each hour as it passes, I shall not be able to prepare for publication on my return home any clear or satisfactory account of these wonders."[18]

Langford added, "So Jake may go to...." but he was too prim to use the word *hell*.

Langford also watched Lieutenant Doane come out of the tent with his hand and forearm thrust into a bucket of ice-cold water. "I am afraid," Langford said, "that lockjaw will set in if he does not consent to have the felon lanced."[19]

Lieutenant Doane had spent the morning galloping from one spring to the next to keep the bandage of the felon on his right thumb cold and wet. But there were no springs as he began to ride along the canyon, and his pain became so intense that he couldn't even remember arriving at Cascade Creek.

"I abandoned my horse," he said, "and have no distinct recollection of how I got to the water's edge, but presently found myself with my arm up to the elbow in the Yellowstone a few yards below the foot of a graceful cascade."[20]

Although Doane thought he soaked his arm in the Yellowstone River, that is unlikely. He said, "I had descended the canyon to a point where the creek joined the river, precipitated into a gorge just above its juncture in a lovely cascade of three falls in aggregate one-hundred feet high." He was describing Cascade Creek before it makes a vertical plunge of 129 feet into the canyon between the Upper and Lower Yellowstone Falls as Crystal Falls.

On August 31, the explorers were so impressed with the Yellowstone Canyon and Fall they decided to spend the whole day exploring them. Washburn went to the area above the falls where he said the river was "flowing peacefully and quiet."[21] About a quarter-mile above the Upper Fall, the river breaks into rapids and foams into eddies around huge boulders. Langford, who also explored above the falls, said, "Above the rapids the river is about one-hundred and fifty yards wide, but, as it approaches the falls, high, rocky bluffs crowd in on both sides, forcing the water into a narrow gorge, which, at the brink of the falls, is about thirty yards wide."[22]

The men went to a ledge just below the Upper Fall that was so close they could feel occasional drops of water on their faces. Langford described the setting:

The river comes down for over half a mile above over a series of lava ledges, each terminating in a fall of from ten to fifteen feet; of these there are five. Then with a tremendous current, and confined in a rocky channel, narrowed to a space of eighty feet, it is hurled from the brink of a perpendicular wall, a sheer descent of one-hundred-fifteen feet. So rapid is the current that mass of foam shoots out clear of the rock and falls far out in its basin, striking upon a covered ledge at an angle which causes a portion of the water to be projected like a broad fan into the air, with a hissing sound to the distance of sixty feet, and afterward dissolving into clouds of spray.[23]

Washburn described the canyon between the Upper and Lower Falls:

The river again resumes its peaceful career. The pool below the falls is a beautiful green capped with white. On the right hand side a clump of pines grew just above the falls, and the grand amphitheater, worn by the maddened waters on the same side, is covered with a dense growth of the same. The left side is steep and craggy. Towering above the falls, half way down and upon a level with the water, is a projecting crag, from which the falls can be seen in all their glory. No perceptible change can be seen in the volume of water here from what it was where we first struck the river. At the head of the rapids are four apparently enormous boulders standing as sentinels in the middle of the stream. Pines are growing upon two of them. From the Upper Fall to the Lower there is no difficulty in reaching the bottom of the canyon. The Lower Falls are about half a mile below the Upper, where the mountains again, as if striving for the mastery, close in on either side, and are not more than seventy feet apart.[24]

The men watched the Upper Falls for more than an hour. Then they went through thick timber about a half-mile down the river to the Lower Falls. Walter Trumbull described them this way:

The plunge of the water is in the direct course of the stream, and at the brink of the falls it appears to be of uniform depth. It clears its bed at a bound, and takes a fearful leap of three-hundred-fifty feet. Having passed over the precipice, the clear, unbroken, greenish mass is in an instant transformed by the jagged edges of the precipice into many streams, apparently separated, yet still united, and having the appearance of molten silver. These streams, or jets, are shaped like a comet, with nucleus and trailing coma, following in quick succession; or they look like foaming, crested tongues, constantly overlapping each other. The outer jets decrease in size as they descend, curl outward, and break into mist. In the sunlight, a rainbow constantly spans the chasm. The foot of the falls is enveloped in mist, which conceals the river for more than a hundred yards below.[25]

Some members of the Washburn Expedition thought the Upper Falls of the Yellowstone, which drop water 109 feet, were more beautiful than the more dramatic Lower Falls at 308 feet.

Below the Lower Fall was the Grand Canyon of the Yellowstone that Washburn described as "a fearful chasm." Langford described the canyon like this:

The Great Falls are at the head of one of the most remarkable canyons in the world—a gorge through volcanic rocks fifty miles long, and varying from one thousand to nearly five thousand feet in depth. In its descent through this wonderful chasm the river falls almost three thousand feet. At one point, where the passage has been worn through a mountain range, our hunters assured us it was more than a vertical mile in depth, and the river, broken into rapids and cascades, appeared no wider than a ribbon. The brain reels as we gaze into this profound and solemn solitude. We shrink from the dizzy verge appalled, glad to feel the solid earth under our feet, and venture no more, except with forms extended, and faces barely protruding over the edge of the precipice. The stillness is horrible. Down, down, down, we see the river attenuated to a thread, tossing its miniature waves, and dashing, with puny strength, the massive walls which imprison it. All access to its margin is denied, and the dark gray rocks hold it in dismal shadow. Even the voice of its waters in their convulsive has excited, and you would rise from your agony cannot be heard.[26]

To explore the bottom of the canyon, Lieutenant Doane and Private George McConnell wended their way through thick forest for three miles down game trails until they came to a stream that ran into the canyon. They tied their horses and waded down the stream bed. As the pair headed down the stream canyon, they encountered sulfur-belching hot springs. One of the springs had built up an enormous horn of sulfur with water trickling down its sides.

The creek ran over a bed of solid rock that was smooth and slippery. The men waded down the treacherous creek for three miles until they came to a shelf in the canyon wall where they found a large flock of bighorn sheep. McConnell shot one of the sheep, but the rest scrambled away on the canyon walls with alacrity that astonished Lieutenant Doane. Below the shelf, the creek headed downward sharply, so Doane and McConnell had to climb down even more carefully.

They scrambled over masses of rock and fallen timber and splashed through the warm water and ducked under cascades that fell from shelves in the canyon wall. They skirted around boiling cauldrons where hot springs bubbled up from the creekbed. The pair toiled downward for four hours before reaching the bottom of the canyon. They were wet, exhausted, and famished with thirst, but the river water was warm and impregnated with alum and sulfur, so it was hard to drink.

The side of the canyon was riddled with springs, some that left deposits of calcium and others of sulfur. These springs came in black, blue, and red. Doane said the canyon floor was oppressively hot despite a stiff breeze that blew constantly down the canyon. He said, "A frying sound comes constantly to the ear, mingled with the rush of the current. The place abounds in sickening and purgatorial smells."[27]

Doane and McConnell had traveled four miles down the creek and could look up the canyon wall to the sky at the edge of the canyon. Tall trees there looked just two or three feet high. Doane said sunlight didn't reach the bottom of the canyon, and when the men looked up they could see stars twinkling in the sky.

Doane said the canyon's depth where they stood "was not less than 2,500 feet and more probably 3,000 feet. There are perhaps other canyons longer and deeper than this one, but surely none combining the grandeur and immensity with peculiarity of formation and profusion of volcanic or chemical phenomena."[28]

It took Doane and McConnell five hours to climb the canyon and reach the place where they had tied their horses. It was dark then, and they had to negotiate dense forest filled with fallen timber, marshes, and hot springs. Langford decided to head straight toward camp without seeking a trail. He and McConnell threaded the marshes where their horses might sink up to their bellies with great caution. They got back to camp at eleven o'clock, wet and chilled to the bone.

Doane, who was still suffering from the infection on his hand, said, "To me it was terribly fatiguing after the excitement passed away, as I was becoming very weak from continued loss of rest or sleep."[29]

There were reports of other members of the expedition getting to the bottom of the canyon, but they are brief and inconsistent. Langford said Sam Hauser and Ben Stickney succeeded about two miles below the falls and estimated the depth there at 1,190 feet. Why Langford would neglect Doane and McConnell's descent of the canyon is unclear. General Washburn said, "Hauser, Stickney and Doane succeeded in reaching the bottom, but it was a dangerous journey."[30] Perhaps Washburn conflated two trips and failed to mention McConnell because he was a mere private.

The spectacular Grand Canyon and Falls of the Yellowstone apparently met—even exceeded—the explorers' expectations. Their descriptions of them were effusive, and the entire group spent a day and a half exploring them, more than they spent at any other feature on their trip.

The evening after the men arrived at the Great Falls of the Yellowstone on August 30, Jake Smith commented, "Well, boys, I have seen all there is and am ready to move on." Langford[31] apparently didn't see the humor in Smith's comment and thought the businessman had actually rejected nature's invitation to stay. But everybody else ignored the joke and spent the next day exploring the areas' wonders.

By September 1, the men knew they had to leave. They could see their supplies dwindling, and they didn't know how long it would take them to get back to civilization.

CHAPTER FIVE

Everts Gets Lost

THE NEXT LEG OF THE TRIP WOULD TAKE THE PARTY PAST GRAND SIGHTS and deadly dangers. They would see scalding steam hissing from fissures on the sides of mountains. They would feel thin crusts crack under their feet as they tried to collect specimens of pure sulfur crystal from the rims of boiling hot springs. They would see giant gobs of hot mud hurled from an earthen cone so large it reminded them of a volcano. And men could get lost while they struggled through tangles of fallen timber and dense forests of living trees.

The explorers had been recruited for their prestige and writing ability, not their outdoor skills. Of General Henry D. Washburn's men, only War-ren Gillette, who had been a freight wagon driver and toll road builder, was an experienced outdoorsman. The others were public officials, lawyers, and businessmen.

The soldiers in the Army escort patrolled vast areas of eastern Montana, so they had to have wilderness experience. Their leader, Lieutenant Gusta-vus Doane, grew up in the California gold camps and had a reputation as a superb horseman and a deadly shot with a rifle.

The tax assessor, Truman Everts, seemed particularly unsuited for wilder-ness travel. At fifty-four, he was the oldest member of the expedition. More important, Everts was so nearsighted that he couldn't recognize a friend from five feet away without his glasses. His eyesight would make following com-panions' tracks through the wilderness nearly impossible.

Ready for arduous travel or not, the explorers knew they had to leave the falls on their third day there. Their supplies were dwindling, and they had to have enough to get back to civilization.

Langford described September 1, the morning they left, this way: "The laughing waters of the Upper Fall were filled with the glitter of rainbows and diamonds. Nature, in the excess of her originality, had seemingly determined that this last look should be the brightest, for there was everything in the landscape, illuminated by the rising sun, to invite a longer stay."[1]

The party broke camp and sent the pack train on its way at ten o'clock, but several men stayed behind to admire the canyon and falls one more time. They knew they could catch up to the slow-moving pack train.

Cornelius Hedges went to the brink of the Lower Falls, where he looked down and described the distance as "appalling." He then went to the Upper Falls and climbed to a point below its brink for "the most magnificent view possible." He said the Upper Falls' beauty is very different from the Lower Falls: "Rock seems hard and much darker. Volume of water seems greater and closer."[2]

It was afternoon before the last men left to catch up with the pack train. After traveling a half-mile above the falls, they saw the last vestige of rapids disappear and the river widen to four hundred feet. Its crystal-clear water flowed peacefully between grass-covered banks. The party then crossed Alum Creek, a small stream whose water deposits had dyed its bed black.

Six miles above the falls, they came to a wide valley where elk grazed and waterbirds frolicked in the river. They saw seven white hills standing two to five hundred feet tall in sharp contrast to their green surroundings. Long-dead hot springs had created these hills where mineral-laden water deposited snowy white calcareous material.

Three miles farther along, they came to an area filled with boiling springs. The springs had formed two hills three hundred feet tall and half a mile across. Hot steam poured from scattered fissures on the hills' surfaces and formed pure sulfur crystals around them. When the men climbed the hills, hollow tones echoed under their feet. Sometimes their horses' hooves broke through the crust, and hot steam erupted from the cracked surface.

Boiling springs surrounded the hills in all directions. The most conspicuous spring was an oval twenty feet long and twelve feet wide that was surrounded by a border of scalloped sediment. Langford described it this way: "The regular formation of this border, and the perfect shading of the scallops forming it, are among the most delicate and wonderful freaks of nature's handiwork. They look like an elaborate work of art."[3]

Next came a basin where dozens of hot springs sent up plumes of steam. The springs were filled with bubbling mud of varying colors: white, blue, yellow, pink, and brown. Steam poured through the mud, making bubbles—some of them two feet high—that would explode with a puff of stinking vapor.

The men couldn't drink the water here because it was infused with chemicals, so they traveled five more miles over sagebrush hills and through high grass meadows to a campsite on the banks of the Yellowstone River. The water there still tasted bad, but it was drinkable. That evening, the men noticed their silver pocket watches had turned the color of lead from the sulfurous gases that hung in the air.

THE NEXT DAY, THE MEN DECIDED TO KEEP THEIR CAMP IN PLACE BY THE Yellowstone River and explore nearby springs. True to his passion, Cornelius Hedges decided to try his luck at fishing, but he caught only one large trout. He saw large sulfurous bubbles coming out of fissures in the river bottom and thought later that they had made him sick.

The men surveyed the area and examined hot springs. The largest was forty feet across, rimmed with limestone and filled with a pool of mud that seethed and bubbled. Langford said, "The disgusting appearance of this spring scarcely atone for the wonder with which it fills the beholder."[4] Nearby, two smaller mud cauldrons boiled away. The men must have smelled ripe from their days of hard travel, so when they came to a hot spring filled with sulfurous water, they were tempted to take a bath. But the spring was too hot.

The men crossed a hill and found a small stream of greenish water that came from a cave on the hillside. Langford described it as "a perfect grotto lined with brilliant metallic tones of green, red and black,"[5] with steam that pulsated every ten seconds and sent out waves of water.

The men came to a geyser with an irregular rim. When this geyser was at rest, they could peer far down its sloping sides, watch a pool of water rise halfway up its cone and then belch up a column of steam that rose three hundred feet. As the geyser began erupting, the ground shook and steam hissed through vents on the surrounding hillside. A huge column of water leapt up twenty feet. Lead-colored water overflowed the crater, where it formed miniature stalagmites. This geyser erupted every six hours and then settled deep into its well. Steam vents stopped hissing, and quiet returned.

While surveying these wonders, the men kept hearing booming and thundering that sounded like distant artillery to the Civil War veterans in the group. As they approached the source of these sounds, they saw a huge cone that reminded them of a volcano perched on a pine-covered hillside. There, a crater thirty feet across belched a heavy cloud of steam three hundred feet into the air.

The men climbed the cone and stood on its rim. When wind blew the steam away, they could look down the crater forty feet into a pool of bubbling mud. Every few seconds, a sound arose from deep in the earth and shook the ground. Some of these beats were so violent that their steam clouds could knock a man down. One man ventured too close and was thrown down the outside of the crater. His companions rushed to help him, but he wasn't injured seriously.

Each beat threw up gobs of mud. Some were barrel-sized and leapt as high as a man's head. Smaller gobs sailed over the rim and hung on trees around the crater. A few of them must have sailed three hundred feet to reach distant trees. The men knew the feature was new because they saw pine needles, still green, caked with mud.

The men dubbed the awesome sight the "Mud Volcano." Lieutenant Doane, who was ever mindful of his duty to write a detached factual report for his Army superiors, said, "It was with difficulty we could believe the evidence of our senses, and, only after the most careful measurements, could we realize the immensity of this wonderful phenomenon."[6]

After Doane saw the Mud Volcano, his felon, the infected abscess on his thumb, hurt so much that he had to return to camp. Langford had been begging Doane to let him lance the felon, but the lieutenant was reluctant. Langford had chloroform in his kit, and Doane wanted to be unconscious for the surgery. Langford told Doane he would use the chloroform, but he didn't really plan to do that. "I am too much of a novice in the business to administer it,"[7] he conceded in his journal.

Langford usually took a lancet when he traveled, but he had left it behind this time. To prepare for surgery, he sharpened his penknife all day on the leather pommel of his saddle as he rode along.

THE MEN WOKE EARLY ON THE MORNING OF SEPTEMBER 3 TO FIND HEAVY frost on their bedding. They were at an elevation of more than seven thousand feet, so freezing weather was no surprise, even in late summer.

While the others prepared to move, Langford and Washburn backtracked along the trail to take another look at the Mud Volcano and the hot springs in the area. Probably Langford wanted more information for articles he planned to write, and Washburn for maps from the Montana Territory Surveyor General's Office.

Langford decided to collect samples of the beautiful alum crystals that surrounded a spring they found. He didn't know that boiling water had undermined the edge of the spring, leaving only a thin crust over it. When he walked toward the pool, the ground began to crack under his feet. Washburn shouted a warning and Langford fell backward. He distributed his weight over the thin crust and rolled carefully to safety. This wouldn't be the last time a warning from the general would save Langford's life.

After Langford and Washburn's survey of the hot springs and Mud Volcano, they returned to camp and discovered the rest of the party had crossed the Yellowstone River and headed south. The pair soon came to an earthworks on the riverbank that showed people had visited the area long ago. Apparently, trappers had built it as a blind where they could hide to shoot geese and ducks on the river.

Langford and Washburn continued to follow the main party's trail. It was easy for two miles, but then an impassable canyon blocked the way, so they turned left to go over the summit of a wooded ridge. They crossed a marshy plain but were forced back to avoid a labyrinth of impassable deadfall. Eventually, they made their way to the shore of Yellowstone Lake.

Langford and Washburn arrived at their camp in a grove by a wide sandy beach. Langford said, "There lay the silvery bosom of the lake, reflecting the beams of the setting sun, and stretching away for miles."[8]

After supper, Hedges went fishing and caught four large trout.

DOANE'S SONOROUS SNORES GREETED THE MEN ON THE MORNING OF SEPtember 4. The lieutenant was sleeping soundly for the first time in nine days because Langford had lanced his felon the night before. Doane finally agreed to the surgery after his hand had swollen so much that he was in constant, severe pain. For days he had been running around looking for frigid springs into which he could plunge his hand and numb his pain. But that—and the opiates he took—didn't work anymore. Even the slightest movement hurt so bad that he could hardly walk.

Langford recruited two strong men to hold Doane down. When the men were in position, Doane asked, "Where's the chloroform?"[9] Langford confessed that he wasn't sure he could administer the drug safely and wasn't going to use it. The lieutenant swallowed his disappointment and laid his hand on an ammunition box.

The men grabbed the lieutenant and held him down. Langford shoved his penknife blade into the bloated thumb and slit it to the end. According to Langford, "Doane gave one shriek as the released corruption flew out in all directions upon the surgeon and his assistants."[10] Then a broad smile lit up Doane's face and he exclaimed, "That was elegant."

Langford applied a poultice to Doane's hand, and the lieutenant soon dropped off to a peaceful sleep. The men decided to let him rest and not move the camp until he awoke.

When Jake Smith heard about the delay, he exclaimed, "If we're going to remain in camp, let's have a game of draw."[11] While the others played poker, Langford used the day to rest and catch up with his journal.

DOANE AWOKE ABOUT NINE O'CLOCK ON THE MORNING OF SEPTEMBER 5 after sleeping for thirty-six hours, and the expedition decided to move on. Langford and Hedges tarried behind to estimate how far they were from the Teton Mountains. They could see the peaks, but they failed to triangulate the distance.

The party passed hot springs on the shore of Yellowstone Lake and marveled at its beauty. They stopped once to watch winds lash the lake into a raging sea with four-foot waves crashing against the beach. The day before, the lake had been calm and glittered in the sunlight and reflected the surrounding pine forests and towering mountains.

After traveling along the lakeshore and making their way over a ridge covered with live pine and deadfall, the party came to a beach covered with oddly shaped rocks that looked like spoons, teacups, pencils, stockings, and amputated body parts such as legs and feet. They named the place "Curiosity Point."

Looking across the lake, they could see huge columns of steam rising from hot springs on the shore of the West Thumb. Later, the men would choose those columns as a rendezvous point where they would wait for any companion who got lost.

The expedition traveled fifteen miles and camped in a beautiful little valley near the lakeshore between a meadow and a beach. After supper, the men combed the beach, finding quartz crystals and carnelian, a brownish-red gemstone.

That night the party voted six to three to continue southward rather than retrace their steps and travel along the west side of Yellowstone Lake. The decision took them away from the relatively easy travel through the Hayden Valley and propelled them toward long stretches of swampy bogs, close-growing live pines, and tangled deadfall that made travel nearly impossible. Had they brought an experienced guide with them, they could have avoided this.

THE EXPEDITION BROKE CAMP AT 10:30 ON THE MORNING OF SEPTEMBER 6 and started southeast along the lakeshore. Soon the party came to marshy land that forced them to strike through a forest where fallen timber made travel almost impossible.

Langford and Doane took a side trip to the top of the highest mountain they could see. Halfway up the slope, they found steaming fissures and rivulets of warm water impregnated with sulfur. The air stank, and hollow sounds echoed under their horses' feet.

The pair rejoined the others and traveled with them. Fallen timber blocked the trail through the forest several times and forced the travelers back to the lakeshore, where their horses' hooves sank in the beach sand, making travel difficult. The party crossed a swampy valley where numerous pools of water were home to thousands of ducks, geese, and swans. The muddy surface of the marsh supported the horses' weight, but their hooves sank down, and they left deep tracks.

Doane said, "The ground was trodden by thousands of elk and sheep. Bear tracks and beaver trails were also numerous."[12] He added that there was even an occasional mountain lion track.

After ten miles of hard travel, the party camped at a marshy spot where the Yellowstone River flowed into the southeast arm of the lake. It was on rough ground in thick timber where there was no grazing for the horses. One man called it the "poorest camp we have had."

That night, mountain lion screams startled the men from their sleep. The shrill sounds were so humanlike that at first the men thought they were from a distressed traveler calling for help.

THE NEXT MORNING, THE MEN FOUND LION TRACKS THAT ENCIRCLED THE camp. The also discovered it was too marshy where they were camped to get across the Yellowstone River, so most of them headed upstream to search for a ford. Langford and Doane decided to climb a nearby mountain to map Yellowstone Lake and to see if they could spot a route to the Grand Geysers on the Firehole River. Langford said he wasn't afraid of encountering Indians. He thought—erroneously—that they feared geysers and hot springs.

Langford and Doane rode around the base of the mountain for three miles and turned up a wooded ravine, then rode for another three miles. They had to dismount and lead their horses around huge rocks and fallen timber. When they reached a point where it was no longer safe to ride, they led their horses.

The slope was so steep that they had to stop often to let the horses catch their breath. When they reached the timberline, they tied their horses and continued to climb an even steeper slope. The men crossed rockslides where they had to step cautiously to avoid tumbling down the mountain. They reached the mountaintop after climbing for four hours.

Langford said, "The view from the summit of this mountain, for wild and rugged grandeur, is surpassed by none I ever before saw. The Yellowstone basin and the Wind River Mountains were spread out before us like a map.

"On the south the eye followed the source of the Yellowstone above the lake, until, twenty-five miles away, it was lost in an immense canyon, beyond which two immense jets of vapor rose to a height of probably three hundred feet. On the north the outlet of the lake and the steam from the mud geyser and mud volcano were distinctly visible."[13]

Doane used his aneroid barometer to estimate the elevation of the peak at 10,327 feet. Up that high, it was freezing cold and the men saw a permanent snow patch thirty feet deep.

It took Langford and Doane an hour and a half to go down the mountain and find their companions' trail. At a fork in the trail, they saw a tripod of poles, an Indian-style direction marker that told them to go to the right.

They followed the trail into a pine forest that was free from underbrush and fallen timber, but darkness soon overtook them and they lost their way. The men built a fire for light to examine tracks on the trail and discovered they had been following an elk herd that crossed their companions' path.

Langford said, "A night on the mountain, without supper or blankets, was not to be endured. We retraced our route to the base of the mountain, and struck out boldly in the darkness for the beach of the lake, where we supposed our party had camped."[14]

When they reached the lake, they rode along the beach for two miles. About ten o'clock they saw their companions' campfire and shouted a loud "halloo." Their anxious companions were relieved and shouted back, guiding them to the camp.

That night, the party decided to name the mountain the pair had climbed "Mount Langford," in honor of the first person to reach its top.[15]

ON SEPTEMBER 8, THE MEN SAW A RIDGE THAT CAME DOWN FROM THE mountains and created a peninsula extending far into the lake, dividing the southeast arm from the south arm. The men decided it would be easier to cross the ridge than to travel many miles on the beach around the peninsula.

When they got to the ridge, they encountered masses of tangled deadfall that forced them into thick timber. The timber was so closely packed that packhorses often wedged themselves between close-growing trees, and the men had to force the stuck animals backward to free them. Sometimes, the horses' packs burst and the men had to retrieve their contents and repack. That slowed progress greatly.

Often, men separated to look for passable routes. Two men even became lost for a while, but they managed to stumble back to the camp that night by following the lakeshore.

Langford commented in his journal, "I know of nothing that can try one's patience more than a trip of any considerable length by wagon train or pack train through an uninhabited region, and the most amiable of our race cannot pass this ordeal entirely unscathed. Persons who are not blessed with uncommon equanimity never get through such a journey without frequent explosions of temper, and seldom without violence. Even education, gentle training and the sharpest of mental discipline do not always so effectually subdue the passions that they may not be aroused into unwonted fury during a long journey through a country filled with obstructions."[16]

Langford apparently had failed to control his own temper that day. That statement came in his journal after he admitted "scolding" another man for a transgression he declined to explain.

While the men were fighting their way through downed timber and brush, tempers flared, but Langford broke the tension by grandly reciting a line from Lord Byron's narrative poem *Childe Harold's Pilgrimage*: "There is a pleasure in the pathless woods." The contrast between the poem and what the men were experiencing was so extreme that they broke out in uproarious laughter.

THE ANTICS OF ONE OF THE PACKHORSES ALSO LIGHTENED THE MOOD. THE man who sold the undersized horse had said, "He is the kind of animal that drives the whole herd before him."[17] The salesman must have meant the animal would always be exhausted and lag behind the rest of the herd.

The little horse was always getting in trouble. He floundered crossing the Yellowstone River and soaked his pack. He got stuck in the mud of swampy sloughs and waited patiently for the men to pull him out.

While the party was traveling along a ridge, the little horse lost his footing and tumbled down the hill. One man described the feat this way: "He had proven himself the acrobat of the pack-train by turning a number of somersaults backward, down the hill, pack and all; and when found, was astride a log lengthwise, his feet just touching on either side, but either unable to extricate himself, or too proud and patient to make an effort to do so. He consequently very resignedly contemplated his position and surroundings. He was too proud and spirited to betray any emotion, though his situation was undoubtedly distasteful to his feelings."[18]

Langford said, "Our little bronco, with all the spirit necessary, lacks oftentimes the power to scale the tree trunks."[19] Several times the men found him caught over a tree on his belly with his front and back legs dangling. Because of the horse's many mishaps and indomitable spirit, Langford dubbed him "Little Invulnerable."

AT THE END OF THE DAY, THE PARTY CAMPED AT THE SOUTHERNMOST ARM of Yellowstone Lake. They had zigzagged more than fifteen miles to get around obstructions, but they were only seven miles by a straight line from where they had camped the night before. Faces were scratched, clothing was torn, and limbs were bruised from squeezing between saplings and pushing through brush.

Doane noted that green grass, berries, and pine nuts were abundant in the area, but the explorers hadn't seen any game. The men had made such a racket yelling at horses and firing their guns to indicate their locations that they drove away everything for miles around. The lieutenant said the small lakes they passed were "perfectly alive with otter, which may be seen playing upon the surfaces at nightfall by hundreds. Beaver, mink and muskrat are also abundant."[20]

In the evening, when two of the men went to search for a trail, they spotted a mama grizzly and her two cubs. They returned to camp to get their guns, and four others decided to join the hunt, confident that six men could easily bag a single bear. While the men were loading their guns, they discussed what to do with the two cubs when they caught them. Some thought the cubs should be taken back to Helena, but the packers said the idea wouldn't work unless they could be used as pack animals.

The men followed the bears' trail to a thicket but were afraid to enter it in the waning daylight. Referring to a Bible story, Jake Smith commented, "I always considered Daniel a great fool to go into a den of bears."[21] Langford felt obliged to criticize Smith for "lack of scriptural accuracy." The Bible story is about a den of lions, and Daniel did not enter it voluntarily.

In the evening, the fact that two men had been lost during that day prompted discussion of what the group should do if somebody else should go missing. Truman Everts said it would be best for the lost person to head west to the headwaters of the Madison River and follow it downstream to the settlements in the valley, but the party agreed to a different plan. They would rush to the West Thumb of the lake, where hot springs sent up tall columns of steam, and wait there. The men had been seeing the steam columns for days and knew they would be an easy beacon for any lost traveler.

Langford and Hedges stood guard that night. They got hungry and raided the kitchen supplies, where they found two grouse that Gillette had shot with his pistol that day and planned to have for his breakfast. Langford and Hedges cooked and ate the birds. When Gillette asked about his grouse the next morning, the cook said his dog, Booby, must have taken them. Then Langford and Hedges confessed and everyone had a good laugh.

When Jake Smith came in from guard duty, greeting everybody jovially and looking refreshed, Langford suspected he had been sleeping on the job. He even asked one of Doane's soldiers to draw a picture of Smith peacefully slumbering.

THE PARTY BROKE CAMP AT TWO O'CLOCK ON SEPTEMBER 9 AND HEADED west through close-standing timber and tangled deadfall. Riders managed to guide their horses between the trees, but packhorses often got stuck and packs had to be rearranged.

The party stalled when the travelers came to a log four feet in diameter. Fallen timber prevented them from going around the huge log. To get the horses over, the men led them so their chests were pressed against the log. Then the two strongest men stooped under the front legs of the animals and lifted. Other men placed the horses' front feet over the log, and still others pushed from behind. The men moved twenty horses over the log that way.

The men continued onward, crossing the ridge that divided the Yellowstone and Snake River drainages, and camped at about 2:00 p.m. on the western slope. Everts didn't arrive with the rest of the party, but that didn't cause concern at first because men often went off by themselves to hunt or see the sights. When Little Invulnerable didn't come in, the men began to search for the packhorse and to watch for Everts. They found Little Invulnerable resting against a tree two miles back, but there was no sign of the missing man.

Toward evening, the men began to worry about Everts. They knew he was extremely nearsighted and would have a tough time following their trail through the deadfall and thick timber even in daylight, a task that would be impossible for him after dark.

The men yelled and fired guns to help Everts find their camp, but the fifty-four-year-old tax assessor never arrived. The next morning, the men launched efforts to find him; their searches lasted until their food started to run out.

CHAPTER SIX

Everts's Ordeal

ON SEPTEMBER 9, THE MEN SEPARATED TO FIND THEIR WAY THROUGH A dense pine forest filled with tangled deadfall. Late that afternoon Truman Everts strayed out of sight of the others as he searched for a route. That didn't bother him because such separations happened all the time. Everts said, "I rode on, fully confident of soon rejoining the company or of finding their camp."[1]

He saw Hedges's packhorse, Little Invulnerable, resting in a clearing and tried to drive the diminutive horse ahead of him, but the tired animal wouldn't budge. Everts gave him up and rode on. Darkness fell, and Everts couldn't find his way, but he wasn't alarmed. He said, "I had no doubt of being with the party at breakfast the next morning. I selected a spot for comfortable repose, picketed my horse, built a fire, and went to sleep."[2]

At dawn, Everts saddled his horse, mounted, and headed in the direction where he supposed the party went. He thought his companions probably had camped overnight on the beach and in the morning headed toward Yellowstone Lake through the thick forest. It was dark under the trees, and fallen pine needles obscured the trail, so the nearsighted man got off his horse often to scrutinize the ground for tracks.

He came to an opening where he could see several possible routes, dismounted, and, leaving his horse unhitched, walked a hundred feet into the forest to look for clues about which way to go. When he returned, the horse was gone with Everts's blankets, rifle, pistols, fishing tackle, and matches. All he had were the things in his pockets: paper and pencil, two small knives, and a small opera glass.

It still didn't occur to Everts that he might never find his companions. He searched for his horse for half a day and finally gave up. Then he wrote notes and hung them in trees to tell his companions the direction he was taking. As he traveled along, he started to worry about another night in the

Truman C. Everts, a nearsighted tax collector, wandered away from the Washburn Expedition with only the items in his pockets. He was rescued after thirty-seven days.

Truman Everts wandered away from the Washburn Expedition near the south-east arm of Yellowstone Lake. The expedition searched for him until their supplies ran low.

wilderness, this one with no matches for a fire or blankets to protect him from the cold at the seven-thousand-foot elevation. Everts said, "I began to realize that my condition was one of actual peril."[3]

He tried not to think about the danger, sitting on a log to reconstruct every foot he had traveled after leaving his companions and to try to determine where they were likely to be. He thought they probably were close and had started to look for him, but they would not find him that night. He decided to sleep next to a fallen log with neither a fire nor a blanket.

He later said, "At no time during my period of exile did I experience so much mental suffering from the cravings of hunger as when, exhausted with this long day of fruitless search, I resigned myself to a couch of pine foliage in the pitchy darkness of a thicket of small trees."[4]

As he lay in the darkness, wind sighed through the tall pines, and the forest seemed alive with owls, coyotes, and wolves. "These sounds, familiar by their constant occurrence throughout the journey," Everts said, "were now full of terror, and drove slumber from my eye-lids. Above all this, however, was the hope that I should be restored to my comrades the next day."[5]

After a night of trying to sleep on rough ground with no fire or blanket to keep him warm at the seven-thousand-foot elevation, Everts rose and headed back to the place where he had posted notes for his friends. He got there about noon and found his notes untouched. That's when he realized he was lost.

"Then came a crushing sense of destitution," he said later. "No food, no fire; no means to procure either; alone in an unexplored wilderness, one hundred and fifty miles from the nearest human abode, surrounded by wild beasts, and famishing with hunger."[6]

But Everts's resolve returned quickly. He said, "A moment afterwards I felt how calamity can elevate the mind, in the formation of the resolution not to perish in that wilderness."[7]

He decided to try to intercept his companions by heading down a ridge that ran into the lake. Once he found the shore, he could race ahead of the group that had to move slowly because of its packhorses. Everts began to clamber over fallen logs and make his way through tangled deadfall.

After two days without food, hunger gnawed at his stomach, but he simply told himself, "This won't do."

He said: "Despondency would sometimes strive with resolution for the mastery of my thoughts. I would think of home—of my daughter—and of the possible chance of starvation, or death in some more terrible form."[8]

The sun was still shining when Everts emerged from the forest into an open glade at the end of the peninsula that ran into the lake. In the distance, he could see a spouting geyser that he said "added novelty to one of the grandest landscapes I ever beheld."[9]

He saw otters cavorting and beaver and mink swimming in the still water of the lake. The nearby forest, he said, was filled with songbirds, elk, deer, and mountain sheep. The wildlife was surprised to see him but not afraid. The "grandeur, beauty and novelty would have been transporting," he said, but hunger and fear depressed his mood. "I longed for food, friends and protection."[10]

Everts's fear of Indians waned, and he began hoping friendly Bannocks or Crows would find him. Such Indians, he imagined, would treat him well because they would hope to be rewarded for keeping him safe.

His preoccupation with Indians got the better of him, and he imagined he saw a lone figure paddling a canoe along the shoreline. He rushed to intercept the canoe only to discover he was watching an enormous pelican that "flapped its dragon wings as if in mockery of my sorrow."[11] His disappointment surged. And night was falling again.

While looking for a spot to sleep, Everts pulled up a small green thistle and discovered it had a long, tapered radish-like root. He took a bite and declared it "palatable and delicious." He assured himself this was not an illusion like the paddling Indian on the lake, then settled down to his first meal in four days.

With his hunger sated, Everts looked for a place to sleep. He found a comfortable spot with a pallet of green foliage between two trees and fell into his first deep sleep in days.

He was startled awake by shrill screams that sounded like a person in distress. Everts recognized the sounds. He had heard them dozens of times before and even answered such anguished calls. They were the screeches of a mountain lion.

He grabbed a nearby branch and swung into a tree, then scrambled up branch by branch until the trunk began to sway under his weight.

The lion sniffed the spot where Everts had been sleeping and growled. Everts answered every growl by screaming at the top of his voice. He broke off branches and threw them at the beast.

The hurled branches didn't bother the lion, and it began to circle the tree as if looking for a place to spring upward. Everts trembled so much that he made the tree's leaves rustle. The lion circled below, roaring, with his tail lashing the ground. It was too dark to see, but the animal's noise told Everts where it was.

Everts said, "Whenever I heard it on one side of the tree I speedily changed to the opposite—an exercise which, in my weakened state, I could only have performed under the impulse of terror. I would alternately sweat and thrill with horror at the thought of being torn to pieces and devoured by this formidable monster."[12]

Everts noticed that his efforts to scare the lion weren't working, so he decided to try being quiet. He grabbed the tree trunk with both arms and repressed his trembling.

The lion started to range around the area, pausing now and then to sniff and scream, making the forest echo. Suddenly, the giant cat fell silent. That frightened Everts even more than the roaring had. Now he couldn't tell where the creature was, and he imagined it would attack anytime. The moments seemed like hours to Everts, but at last the lion ran screaming into the forest.

Everts wanted to stay in the tree but was too tired to hang on. He was so weak that he had difficulty climbing down, but he managed. Soon he was lying where he first heard the lion scream, and he fell into a deep sleep. He didn't wake until the sun was up.

The encounter with the lion seemed like a dream, but Everts knew it was real because he could see the broken tree branches he had thrown at the beast and the places where it had tromped down the grass. Everts shuddered when he thought about the lion. He wondered if another animal would attack him, or if hostile Sioux Indians would torture him to death, or if he would just die of starvation. He thought about his family and how they might cope with never knowing what happened to him.

A cold wind penetrated Everts's tattered clothes and broke his reverie. He could see the wind rising to a gale that would bring cold and snow. While he stood in the falling snow, he saw a small bird benumbed by the frigid weather. "I instantly seized and killed it, and, plucking its feathers, ate it raw. It was a delicious meal for a half-starved man."[13]

Everts knew he had to find better shelter than the branches of the spruce tree he was standing under. When the mix of rain and snow paused, he headed toward columns of steam he saw in the distance hoping to find warmth there. After walking ten miles he came to a cluster of hot springs and lay down under a tree near them. He felt warmth spread through his body, but he left his feet in the cold, and they became frostbitten.

As soon as his chill abated, he got up and harvested a mess of thistle roots that grew in abundance nearby, ate enough to fill his stomach, and saved the rest for later.

He found a spot between two boiling springs that were far enough apart to keep his head and feet warm at the same time. Nearby was a smaller spring where he could cook his gathered roots.

He ripped branches off pines and built a bower between the springs. After he spread a layer of small branches and fallen foliage on the ground inside his shelter, he crawled in to wait out the storm, which eventually dropped two feet of snow.

Everts said, "The vapor which supplied me with warmth saturated my clothing with its condensations. I was enveloped in a perpetual steam bath.

At first this was barely preferable to the storm, but I soon became accustomed to it, and before I left, though thoroughly parboiled, actually enjoyed it."[14]

While hunkered down in his shelter, he had nothing to do except sleep, cook, and think about a means of escape. He wished for a companion to share his misery: "What a relief it would be to compare my wretchedness with that of a brother sufferer, and with him devise expedients for every exigency as it occurred!"[15]

He mulled over ideas for improving his situation. Nothing concerned him more than figuring out a way to build a fire to warm him on cold nights, to cook food, and to scare away wild animals at night. He looked out and saw sunlight gleaming on the lake and "with it the thought flashed upon my mind that I could, with a lens from my opera-glasses, get fire from heaven.

"I felt, if the whole world were offered me for it," he said. "I would cast it all aside before parting with that little spark. I was now the happy possessor of food and fire. These would carry me through."[16]

On Everts's third night in his pine bower, he rolled over and broke the thin crust where he slept. Steam poured out of the crack and scalded his hip.

Everts didn't waste time while he waited for the heavy snow to melt. He made a knife by sharpening a buckle from his vest, and he used it to cut leather from his boots to make slippers for his frostbitten feet. He cut up a linen handkerchief and mended his torn clothing. He made a fishhook from a pin he found in his coat. He cut the tops off his boots and sewed up the bottoms to make pouches for carrying food.

Eight days after coming to the spring, Everts packed his new pouches with thistles and headed toward the southeast arm of Yellowstone Lake. He said, "The sun shone bright and warm, and there was a freshness in the atmosphere truly exhilarating."[17]

As he walked along, Everts thought of his daughter and family. It occurred to him that the storm and diminishing food supplies probably had forced his companions to abandon any search for him. "The thought was full of bitterness and sorrow—I tried to realize what their conjectures were concerning my disappearance; but could derive no consolation from the long and dismal train of circumstances they suggested."[18]

Everts realized that his lack of nutritious food was affecting his mind. He said he could think well enough for self-preservation but "was in a condition to receive impressions akin to insanity. I was constantly traveling in dream-land, and indulging in strange reveries such as I had never before known."

A cold wind chilled Everts, so he pulled out his lens and some dry wood, but the overcast sky kept him from starting a fire. He sat on a log to wait for the sun to come out. Soon, darkness came instead, and he faced another night without fire. "A bleak hillside sparsely covered with pines afforded poor accommodations for a half clad, famished man," he said. The only way he could stay warm was by walking and striking his numb hands and feet on fallen logs. At dawn, he headed back to his bower by the hot springs and built a fire. He stayed there for two days.

He felt sure his companions had given up their search for him, so he would have to get to civilization on his own. He considered which of three routes he could take: south along the Snake River to settlements in Wyoming; west around the end of Yellowstone Lake and across the mountains to the Madison River Valley; or north back along the arduous path that had brought him to where he was.

He decided against turning back because he was familiar with the difficulties there and against going south because he feared the dangers of the Snake River Canyon. He decided to head toward the settlements on the Madison. That was the shortest route, although it required crossing a mountain range. He filled his pouches with thistle roots and started toward Yellowstone Lake.

He traveled all day over piles of fallen trees and through brush thickets. He paused at noon to start a fire with his lens and carried a burning stick the rest of the day so nightfall wouldn't catch him with no way to start a fire. By late afternoon, he felt faint and exhausted, so he stopped at the only open spot he could find to prepare for the coming night.

He was under a canopy of pine branches so dense that no light filtered in from the night sky. He heard night birds shriek, mountain lions scream, and wolves howl. He couldn't lie down because of his scalded hip, so he sat with his back against a tree.

"I vainly tried," he said, "amid the din and uproar of this horrible serenade, to woo the drowsy god. My imagination was instinct with terror. At one moment it seemed as if, in the density of a thicket, I could see the blazing eyes of a formidable forest monster fixed upon me, preparatory to a deadly leap; at another I fancied that I heard the swift approach of a pack of yelping wolves through the distant brushwood, which in a few moments would tear me limb from limb."[19]

Exhaustion overtook him, and he finally fell into a fitful sleep. Then things got worse. "I fell forward into the fire, and inflicted a wretched burn on my hand," he said. "Oh with what agony I longed for day!"

When the "bright and glorious morning succeeded the dismal night,"[20] Everts decided he had been the victim of uncontrolled nervousness and vowed to stop that. With his new resolve, he resumed his journey toward Yellowstone Lake. After a day of hard travel through tall timber and thickets, he found himself on a high ridge overlooking the lake.

"In front of me," he said, "at a distance of fifty miles away, in the clear blue horizon, rose the arrowy peaks of the three Tetons."[21] To his right, he saw the rugged Madison Range, and behind him were the mountains named for him and his companions: Doane and Langford.

Everts said he became so involved in the natural grandeur of the scene that he almost forgot to start a fire. At last, he took out the lens he had harvested from his opera glasses and started a wand burning that he carried for the rest of the day. Eventually, he made his way down a steep slope to the beach, gathered wood, and kindled a blaze.

He found that warm, wet beach sand soothed his frostbitten feet, so he took off his makeshift slippers and hung them on his belt. Then he gathered wood along the shore. After he had enough wood for an overnight fire, he sat for a long time with his feet in the sand. Darkness started to fall, and temperatures began to plummet, so Everts decided to put on his slippers—and discovered one of them was missing!

Fearing a cold night with a bare foot, Everts began a frantic search for the missing slipper. Although he was afraid it had fallen into the lake and washed away, he kept searching. To search in the dark, he pulled flaming brands from his fire so he could see to scour the ground. Finally, he found the slipper. It had been torn from his belt when he scraped past a tree limb.

With a surge of relief, Everts sat in the sand, leaned against a fallen log, and listened to the waves on the beach of Yellowstone Lake. "It was a wild lullaby," he said, "but had no terrors for a worn-out man. I never passed a night of more refreshing sleep."[22]

When Everts awoke, he found his fire had burned down to a few embers, but he soon fanned up a cheerful blaze and ate his breakfast with relish. Then he headed along the beach with optimism, hoping to find a campsite of his companions where there would be food and a note telling where they went.

He did find a campsite, but after a diligent search he couldn't locate a note or any food. He did find a lost dinner fork that would be good for digging roots and a can that had once held yeast powder, which he could use for a drinking cup and dinner pot. He later learned that his companions had cached food for him in several places.

Everts left the campsite feeling dejected and followed his companions' trail. When the sun was high, he started a fire with his opera glass lens and carried a burning brand to his camp that night. He made a fire and built a bower of pine boughs to protect himself from a violent wind that was lashing the lake to foam.

He awoke to the snapping and crackling of burning foliage and found his makeshift bower and the nearby woods aflame. As he made his escape, flames burned his left hand and singed his hair and beard. The fire also destroyed the things he had made while waiting out the snowstorm between hot springs: a buckle-tongue knife, a pin fishhook, and a tape fish line.

He said he had never seen anything "so terribly beautiful" as the blazing forest. "An immense sheet of flame, following to their tops the lofty trees of an almost impenetrable pine forest, leaping madly from top to top, and sending thousands of forked tongues a hundred feet or more athwart the midnight darkness, lighting up with lurid gloom and glare the surrounding scenery of lake and mountains, fills the beholder with mingled feelings of awe and astonishment."[23]

Fanned by the still powerful wind, the fire jumped from tree to tree. The sound of breaking limbs and falling trees was deafening. The entire hillside soon was an ocean of fire. It left behind a blackened scar where only smoking tree trunks rose like ghosts above the smoldering ground.

The fire obliterated any hope of finding his companions' trail, so Everts decided his best hope was to make for the headwaters of the Madison River and follow it down to the ranches there. He looked for the lowest notch in the Madison Mountain Range and made a plan to reach it.

He struggled all day through thickets, tangles of fallen timber, and thick forest, using the notch as his beacon. The farther he traveled, the more the notch seemed to recede in the distance. By nightfall, he was only halfway there, so he built a fire and slept. He was up before dawn to continue his trek.

He came to the base of the mountains and looked up at the formidable succession of rocky peaks and precipices. Sheer walls of gray rock rose up hundreds of feet and blocked his way. He knew he was less than twenty miles from the Madison drainage, and following it for thirty miles would bring him to ranches where he would find friendship and food, so he decided to spend a full day looking for a pass through the forbidding landscape.

He had left the lake with only a few of the thistle roots that provided his only food, so he decided to replenish his dwindling supply. Alas, none were to be found.

While Everts pondered whether he should keep looking for a passage to the Madison headwaters or head back along the Yellowstone, strange thoughts entered his head. He called what he was experiencing "strange hallucinations," but he always denied that he lost his mind. Probably starvation was affecting him; his diet of thistle roots had little nutritional value.

He said an apparition appeared to him: "An old clerical friend, for whose character and counsel I had always cherished peculiar regard, in some unaccountable manner seemed to be standing before me, charged with advice which would relieve my perplexity."[24]

His old friend had a message for him: "Go back immediately, as rapidly as your strength will permit. There is no food here, and the idea of scaling these rocks is madness."[25]

Everts argued that he was far closer to help along the Madison "just over these rocks, a few miles away. As a last trial, it seems to me I can but attempt to scale this mountain or perish in the effort, if God so wills."[26]

The clerical apparition replied, "Don't think of it. Your power of endurance will carry you through. I will accompany you. Put your trust in Heaven. Help yourself and God will help you."[27] With that, Everts decided to turn back, delighted to have a travel companion.

Sometimes as he traveled along, he would start to doubt the wisdom of turning back, but his old friend would reappear and tell him to go on. As he struggled through the forests, he started to wonder if it wouldn't be better just to lie down and die, but there was a whisper in the air: "Where there's life, there's hope."

It took Everts four days to get back to where the Yellowstone River flowed into the lake, and it was only then that he found thistle roots to eat.

One day, he found the tip of a seagull wing on the ground. It was fresh, so he promptly made a fire, mashed the wing to a powder and made a broth in the yeast can he carried.

Everts lost track of time, and the pain dissipated from his many injuries—frostbitten feet, burned hands, a scalded hip, and festering sores on the joints of his fingers. His diet of thistle roots lodged in his gut, and he was constipated. He knew he was starving, but in his sleep he dreamed of "the choicest dishes known to the modern cuisine, and in my disturbed slumbers would enjoy with epicurean relish the food thus furnished even to repletion."[28]

The day he reached Yellowstone Falls was overcast, cold, and windy, so Everts wanted to build a fire. He said, "I had no heart to gaze upon a scene which a few weeks before had inspired me with rapture and awe. One moment of sunshine was of more value to me than all the marvels amid which I was famishing."[29] But the sun refused to shine and he spent the night shivering in a thicket.

He awaited the morning sun with his lens ready, "kindled a mighty flame," and sat by its warmth for several hours. He said, "The great falls of the Yellowstone were roaring within three hundred yards, and the awful canyon yawned almost at my feet; but they had lost all charm for me."[30]

Everts's clerical friend left him, but he still had hallucinations. His body parts began to complain to him. His legs demanded rest, and his stomach demanded a change of diet.

He found a warm stream coming from a spring that was swarming with minnows he could catch with his hands. He scooped them up and ate them raw, but his stomach protested, and he threw them up.

As Everts's body weakened, so did his will to live. "Starving, foot-sore, half blind, worn to a skeleton," he said, "was it surprising that I lacked the faith needful to buoy me above the dark waters of despair, which I now felt were closing around me?"[31]

But he struggled on, sleeping in a hollow tree, trying to catch fish, and thinking of his daughter back home in Helena. He lost his lens and had to backtrack to find it, only to discover a coming snowstorm blocked the sun. He rejoiced when a sunbeam finally came and a "thread of smoke curled gracefully upwards from the Heaven-lighted spark."[32] The next morning, he decided to carry a burning stick with him and not rely on his lens anymore.

"Seizing a brand," he said, "I stumbled blindly on, stopping within the shadow of every rock and clump to renew energy for a final conflict for life."[33]

At last, he became aware of a reflection of burnished steel and saw the kindly faces of two men. He reported conversation with them this way:

"'Are you Mr. Everts?'

"'Yes. All that is left of him.'

"'We have come for you.'

"'Who sent you?'

"'Judge Lawrence and other friends.'

"'God bless him, and them, and you! I am saved!' and with these words, powerless of further effort, I fell forward into the arms of my preservers, in a state of unconsciousness. I was saved."[34]

CHAPTER SEVEN

Searching for Everts

THE MEN KEPT THEIR CAMPFIRES BURNING BRIGHTLY THROUGH THE NIGHT and fired their rifles in hopes of guiding Everts in, but the only replies they heard were the screams of mountain lions that Doane said made a "peculiar, wild and mournful sound."[1] The next morning, the explorers became alarmed and tried to figure out what Everts would do when he discovered he was lost. The nearsighted man, they decided, would give up trying to find their trail and would head to the lakeshore where the beach would provide an unobstructed path and a sure route. That way, Everts could intercept his companions as they made their way around the lake. Everts could travel twice as fast as the others because he was not impeded by the slow pack train.

General Washburn decided not to search the area where Everts went missing. Instead, he sent Gillette and Trumbull back along the lakeshore, where he was sure they would find the missing tax assessor. Gillette packed bread, coffee, and extra blankets to give to the missing man when they found him. Then he and Trumbull headed to where they thought Everts would reach the lake.

The rest of the party broke camp at about 10:00 a.m., hoping to make it that day to the tip of the southwest arm of Yellowstone Lake. That was on the way to the giant steam column where they had agreed to rendezvous if anyone got lost. They were sure Everts would try to catch up with them there, so he would have to pass the southern tip of the lake.

Langford and Hauser left the group and went up a nearby mountain to survey the area. There, Langford climbed a tall tree and saw the west and south shores of Yellowstone Lake. The men built a large fire on the summit where it could be seen for miles to provide a beacon for Everts.

The other explorers had to make their way through tangled timber, and their horses had to jump over fallen logs, so travel was slow. At the end of the day, they were forced to camp on the lakeshore just five miles from where they had been the night before. As night fell, the men started to worry, not just about Everts but also about Gillette and Trumbull, who hadn't returned from their search of the lakeshore.

Gillette and Trumbull returned to the main camp on the morning of September 11. They had gone back as far as the camp of September 9, built fires, put up notices, and left provisions. After a breakfast of bacon cooked on sticks over their campfire and coffee made in tin cups, the pair had searched another four miles up the lakeshore but saw no signs of Everts.

After the explorers heard Gillette and Trumbull's report, everybody was sure Everts had gone to the steam columns on the west side of the lake, so Washburn decided to rush there. By the end of the day, the party reached Yellowstone Lake's West Thumb. Doane described it as "a lovely bay of water, six miles across, and with steam jets rising at its southern extremity in great numbers."[2]

The men gathered around the campfire that night and devised a search plan for the next day. Langford and Washburn would go south to the foot of Brown Mountain, Hauser and Gillette back to the campsite of the day before, and Smith and Trumbull back along the beach. Stickney was to inventory provisions, and Hedges was directed "to lay in a store of fish."[3] Their discussion was interrupted by the scream of a mountain lion that Langford said had "a screech so terribly human, that, for a moment, supposing it to be our missing comrade, we hallooed in response."[4] That was the night Everts scrambled to the top of a tree to get away from a lion that pounced on the spot where he had been sleeping.

While the search parties went out on the morning of September 12, Stickney inventoried the expedition's supplies. He found that their stock of coffee, sugar, and flour was nearly gone and other provisions were very low. When the expedition left Helena, it had a thirty-day supply of food. The travelers had already been gone for twenty-seven days, and getting back would take them at least a week. Stickney figured they could continue searching for Everts for a few more days, but only if they were careful.

Meanwhile, Hedges took his fishing pole to the lake to supplement the expedition's larder. He said his fishing assignment made him "proud of this tribute to my piscatory skill." The attorney also claimed, "There is no body of water under the sun more attractive to the ambitious fisherman than Yellowstone Lake." He proved it by catching fifty fish in less than two hours, "not one of which would weigh less than two pounds, while the average weight was about three pounds."[5]

The Helena attorney also performed another fishing feat that became famous. At a spot where boiling hot springs bubbled away at the edge of the lake, he became the first person to catch a fish and immediately cook it in a hot spring.

He saw several fish near a large spring and "solicited their attention to a transfixed grasshopper, and meeting an early and energetic response."[6]

He said that as he attempted to land his prize, the fish escaped the hook and fell into the boiling water. He got the fish out with his pole and found it cooked clear through. Later travelers would duplicate this feat by dipping a fish still on the hook into a boiling spring, but Hedges thought it was "far too shocking to repeat."[7]

Jake Smith and Walter Trumbull searched for Everts northward along the lakeshore until they came to a place where they could see the previous day's camp. They stopped to eat and unsaddled their horses. Trumbull fished to catch their lunch while Smith took his gun and went ahead to continue the search.

Trumbull had caught four fish and built a fire when Smith came rushing back. Smith calmly announced that he had seen six Indians a mile away, on a point jutting into the lake.

The men abandoned their fish still cooking over the fire, saddled their horses, and rode away to investigate. Trumbull couldn't see the Indians, perhaps because, according to Langford, he was "somewhat nearsighted," but Smith was sure they were "flitting phantom-like among the rocks and trees."[8] Smith and Trumbull made a hasty retreat to camp.

Doane said in his report that they were probably white men. He explained that the explorers later met a group of white men. What Smith saw might have been members of the Sheepeater Band of Shoshone Indians who lived in the area, but Doane's explanation is more likely.

Langford and Washburn headed south toward what they called Brown Mountain, twelve miles away. On their way, they searched for tracks from Everts's horse and concluded that he hadn't passed westward between the mountain and Yellowstone Lake. They didn't know Everts's horse had run away.

On their return trip, Langford said, they passed through a brimstone basin that contained fifty or so hot springs. "We found many small craters from six to twelve inches in diameter, from which issued the sound of the boiling sulfur or mud."[9] Water in the craters was too hot for a man to hold his hand in it for more than three seconds.

A thick green turf that could support a lone man covered the area, but it could give way under the combined weight of a horse and rider. Under the turf was boiling hot mud that wouldn't support any weight.

General Washburn warned Langford to stay away from such places, but his horse broke through and sank to its belly. Langford leapt off and the animal struggled free. Without a man on his back, the horse could walk to safety on the turf.

Later, the turf gave way again. Langford's horse plunged, throwing the man over its head. As Langford landed, he thrust his right arm in front of him. His arm punched through the turf and into the scalding mud. He yanked his arm back and jerked his glove off to keep from blistering his hand.

Langford said, "It is a fortunate circumstance that I today rode my light-weight pack horse; for, if I had ridden my heavy saddle horse, I think that the additional weight of his body would have broken the turf which held up the lighter animal, and that he would have disappeared in the hot boiling mud, taking me with him."[10]

The pair made their way back to camp, where Doane inquired about the white mud that covered the legs of Langford's horse.

GILLETTE AND HAUSER DIDN'T RETURN TO CAMP THAT NIGHT, BUT THEY had been expected to stay out several days searching systematically all the way back to the camp where Everts got lost.

Snow began to fall early in the evening of September 12. Langford said, "Through the hazy atmosphere we beheld, on the shore of the inlet opposite our camp, the steam ascending in jets from more than fifty craters, giving it much the appearance of a New England factory village."[11]

Two feet of snow fell overnight, so the travelers decided to stay put on September 13. Most of the men spent the day playing cards in the pavilion

Warren C. Gillette was the most accomplished outdoorsman in the Washburn Expedition. He stayed behind to search for the missing Truman Everts.

tent, but Lieutenant Doane ventured out by himself to investigate the source of the gigantic steam jets on the West Thumb of the lake. Doane may have hoped Everts was waiting there at their designated rendezvous point, but he doesn't mention that in his journals.

Doane didn't find Everts, but he saw a dramatic collection of geothermal features. The lieutenant, who was always objective and detached in his descriptions, said, "This was the largest system we had yet seen. They embraced every variety of hot water and mud springs seen thus far on the route, with many other heretofore unseen."[12]

Four hundred yards from the lakeshore, Doane found a basin seventy feet in diameter that was filled with thick bubbling mud. The center of the basin was a brilliant pink, but it faded to white at the edges.

Around the basin, Doane found a dozen springs from six to twenty-five feet across that were filled with mud of a paint-like consistency, with colors ranging from pure white to bright yellow. Then came springs of crystal-clear water with an array of colors lining their basins: red, green, yellow, and black.

Closer to the lake were several craters, some of them forty feet across. Water boils at 165 degrees Fahrenheit at the 7,700-foot elevation of Yellowstone Lake, and Doane saw several large springs boiling away.

The usually reserved Doane said, "It is impossible to adequately describe, and utterly impossible to realize from any description, more than a faint idea of the beauties and wonders of this group."[13]

On his way back home, Doane noticed that the fire he and Washburn had set on the top of a nearby mountain to serve as a beacon to Everts was burning out of control. It had spread, he said, "to a vast conflagration, before the devouring flames of which tall pine trees shrivel up and are consumed like grass. The whole summit of the mountain sends up a vast column of smoke which reaches to the sky, a pillar of cloud by day and of fire at night."[14]

Doane returned to camp that evening, "profoundly impressed with the greatness of the phenomena we were witnessing from day to day, and of their probable future importance to science."[15]

That night, hail and snow kept falling. Gillette and Hauser came out of the miserable weather after searching the last six of the party's campsites and reported no sign of Everts. They had examined the expedition's trail, but fallen pine needles obscured it so badly that Gillette figured the nearsighted

Everts could never have followed it. Gillette and Hauser also scoured the beach where Everts might have gone, but they found no trace of the missing man.

When the snow began to fall, Gillette's clothing was still soaked from riding in the rain. The freezing weather made him so cold that he had to borrow Hauser's overcoat. The miserable weather probably helped Hauser persuade Gillette to abandon his plan to continue his search to all of the expedition's previous campsites.

As they returned, the pair lost their way when falling snow obscured visibility and buried the trail. Luckily, the cook's dog, Booby, heard them coming and bounded out to guide them back to camp. Otherwise, Gillette said, they would have spent the night out in the storm.

Gillette and Hauser's report convinced the travelers that Everts could not have followed their trail. They decided Everts must have headed south following the Snake River toward settlements or back down the Yellowstone toward Bottler's ranch.

The snow continued, and the men decided to remain in place for the next two days. They were camped in a spot Everts would have to pass if he headed toward the columns of steam rising on the west side of the lake—the rendezvous point they had agreed on—and they still held out hope that he might find them. But Everts was not searching for his companions. He was waiting out the snowstorm in his wickiup between two hot springs.

IT SNOWED OVERNIGHT AND ALL THROUGH THE DAY OF SEPTEMBER 14. THE accumulation of nearly two feet forced the men to stay in Doane's pavilion tent, playing cards and resting.

Doane borrowed Langford's journal so he could record the events of days he lost while nursing his thumb infection. Langford also worked on his journal. He said, "I am determined to make my journal as full as possible, and to purposely omit no details. It is a lifetime opportunity for publishing to all who may be interested a complete record of the discoveries of an expedition which in coming time will rank among the first and most important of American explorations."[16]

The snow continued overnight, but by midmorning on September 15, a warm west wind blew in. By evening, half the snow had melted, leaving ten inches on the ground.

The expedition's horses were becoming restless because they couldn't find enough grass to eat by pawing through the heavy snow. They had to be tethered on ropes to keep them from wandering away and to protect them from mountain lions that still pierced the air every night with their screams.

In their journals, Langford and Doane commented that the party had seen no Indians despite Jake Smith's report of them on September 12. Langford said, "We feel convinced that Jake Smith drew upon both his imagination and his fears three days ago, when he reported that he had seen Indians on the beach of the lake."[17]

Doane said, "The only traces of Indians we had seen were some shelters of logs, rotten and tumbling down from age, together with a few poles standing in former summer camps; there were no fresh trails whatever."[18] Even the Sheepeater Shoshone appeared to have abandoned the area, he said.

Doane added, "A party of three can travel with perfect safety, so far as Indians are concerned, in any part of this district, by keeping close watch upon their horses at night, as the lions would make short work with them if an opportunity was afforded, horse-flesh being their favorite diet."[19]

The travelers woke early on the morning of September 16 and began packing to move the camp five miles around Yellowstone Lake to the West Thumb. They had been watching huge plumes of steam rising from the hot springs there for days. The snow had melted down to six inches, and the men collected specimens from around the springs. Hedges caught twenty fish to supplement the party's dwindling supplies.

Langford described the situation: "Filled with gloom at the loss of our comrade, tired, tattered, browned by exposure and reduced in flesh by our labors, we resemble more a party of organized mendicants than of men in pursuit of Nature's greatest novelties. But from this point we hope that our journey will be comparatively free from difficulties of travel."[20]

The expedition headed toward the west shore of the West Thumb of Yellowstone Lake. When the men arrived at the hot springs there, Langford was as impressed with them as Doane had been four days before.

"These springs surpass in extent, variety and beauty any which we have heretofore seen," he said. "They extend for the distance of nearly a mile along the shore of the lake, and back from the beach about one hundred yards. They number between ninety and one hundred springs, of all imaginable varieties."[21]

Like Doane, Langford was enthralled with the paint pots of bubbling mud of "various colors, in some cases being dark red, in others scarlet, in others yellow, and in still others green."[22]

Langford also noted the large "dark blue or ultra-marine"[23] springs at the edge of Yellowstone Lake and the hot spring cones that poked above the surface of the water.

Always more expansive in his descriptions than Doane, Langford said, "No camp or place of rest on our journey has afforded our party greater satisfaction than the one we are now occupying."[24]

But as interesting and exciting as the springs were, the party remained gloomy. Langford described the mood: "It is a source of great regret to us all that we must leave this place and abandon the search for Mr. Everts; but our provisions are rapidly diminishing, and force of circumstances obliges us to move forward."[25]

GILLETTE QUESTIONED WASHBURN'S DECISION TO ABANDON THE SEARCH for Everts, so the general convened the party to discuss things. Smith made a motion supporting Washburn, and everybody but Gillette voted for it.

Gillette told Washburn he would continue the search if he could get two men to join him. The men were gloomy about the decision to abandon the search for Everts, so Hauser tried to inject some levity into the situation. He called Gillette's request "a pretty good bluff" because nobody would be willing to join him.

Hauser also remarked, "I think that I should be willing to take the risk of spending ten days more in this wilderness, if I thought that by so doing I could find a father-in-law."[26]

That provoked uproarious laughter because everybody knew that Gillette had been courting Everts's daughter, Bessie, who was described as "one of the most attractive of Montana belles."

None of the civilians volunteered to go with Gillette, so General Washburn asked Lieutenant Doane if he had men who would. The lieutenant immediately ordered privates Charles Moore and John Williamson to help Gillette. The search party left camp at the same time the others headed west.

The searchers had no trouble returning to the Snow Camp, but a storm drove them south, where they camped on the shore of Yellowstone Lake. They met a man who told them he was part of a group of four who had come up the Snake River and were camped nearby. Perhaps the man was a prospector, but Gillette suspected he was a fugitive from justice because of his "repressed nervous manner."[27] Gillette told the man about Everts, presumably hoping for help in the search. The searchers had an evening meal of fish and a grouse that Gillette had killed with his pistol, and they bedded down in rain that lasted all night.

The weather looked good the next morning, but after a while, a drenching rain began to fall. Williamson went hunting while Gillette and Moore made a makeshift shelter out of poles and blankets. When the shelter builders heard shots, Moore went out with a mule and helped Williamson retrieve a fat heifer elk. The men ate elk liver that night.

Over the next two days, the trio backtracked along the route the expedition had traveled and examined their old campsites. They found that the caches of food that had been left for Everts were untouched. On September 9, they arrived at the camp where Everts first went missing and scoured the area for clues of where he might have gone, to no avail.

On the morning of September 21, the searchers saw a storm forming on the nearby mountains. With their food running out and fresh snow likely to obliterate their return trail, they decided to head back to the lake.

Gillette said, "I hated to leave for home, while there was a possibility of finding poor Everts but the chance of our finding him was so very small."[28] He still hoped to find the tax assessor had somehow made it to safety in Virginia City or Helena.

Gillette wondered about Everts and still held out hope that he was alive: "Where is the poor man, Everts? Is he alive? Is he dead in the mountains wandering, he knows not whither? or back home safely? Did he kill his horse? If so I wonder how he likes horseflesh? With dried horse meat he could live thirty or forty days. How he must have suffered even at the best!"[29]

With their own food running out, Gillette and his companions rushed back along the route of the rest of the expedition. By September 23, they made it to the Upper Geyser Basin but didn't tarry there long. They rushed down the Madison River Canyon and out into its wide valley.

On September 27, the men were up at sunrise and had a breakfast of elk meat. Gillette commented, "I don't know what we could have done without the elk meat we have used."[30] The men still had fifteen pounds of meat from the elk Williamson had shot on September 18, but they were running out of flour.

Gillette and the two soldiers parted ways. The soldiers headed east back to Fort Ellis, and Gillette returned to Helena, arriving on October 1. Fifteen days later, Jack Baronett found the emaciated Everts and carried him to safety.

When the Washburn Expedition emerged from the area that was to become Yellowstone Park, N. P. Langford rushed ahead of the others to the telegraph office in Virginia City to report the news. The next day, September 24, the *Helena Daily Herald* published a one-paragraph report based on information Langford provided. The *Herald* said, "Members of the expedition spent eight days hunting for him in the mountains, but found no trace of him."

The news disturbed Everts's friends, and on October 6 the *Herald* announced a $600 reward had been offered for his rescue and that two men, John Baronett and George A. Pritchett, had already gone to find him. Little is known about Pritchett, but Baronett, or "Yellowstone Jack" as he was called, was a colorful character whose biography is well documented. At age forty-six, he had already sailed to China and the Arctic and prospected for gold in California and Montana. More important, he had led a prospecting expedition to the Upper Yellowstone in 1866.

Baronett and Pritchett recruited Crow Indians to help them and got ample supplies. They said they planned to keep searching until they found Everts or winter snows drove them back.

Baronett found Everts on October 6. He recalled the encounter far differently than Everts did. Baronett said he heard his dog growl and saw a black object on the ground—a bear, he thought. Baronett's first inclination was to shoot the thing from where he stood, but it was moving so slowly that he decided to walk up and investigate.

"When I got near it I found it was not a bear," he said, "and for my life could not tell what it was. It did not look like any animal that I had ever seen, and certainly was not a human being. It never occurred to me that it was Everts.

"I went up close to the object; it was making a low groaning noise, crawling along upon its knees and elbows, and trying to drag itself up the mountain. Then it suddenly occurred to me that it was the object of my search."[31]

BARONETT PICKED UP THE EMACIATED MAN, WHO WEIGHED NO MORE THAN fifty pounds, and took him to a safer place. Everts's clothing was shredded; the balls of his scalded feet were worn to the bone; his hands were like claws, and his skin was black. Baronett built a fire and fed Everts tea with a spoon before taking him to a camp for the night. The next day, he took Everts to a miner's cabin and cared for him there.

Meanwhile, Baronett's partner, George Pritchett, rushed 150 miles back to Bozeman to get a doctor and a wagon to haul Everts to safety. Pritchett recruited a doctor and four men to help, but they could get their wagon only halfway to Everts because there were no roads into the Yellowstone wilderness.

At the cabin, Baronett nursed Everts with "the solicitude of brotherly love,"[32] but his ministrations didn't help at first, apparently because weeks of surviving on thistle roots had blocked Everts's digestive tract, causing him immense pain and keeping him from eating. Then, an old hunter stopped by the cabin and came up with a cure.

Everts said the hunter "listened to the story of my sufferings, and tears rapidly coursed each other down his rough, weather-beaten face. But when he was told of my present necessity, brightening in a moment, he exclaimed:

"'Why, Lord bless you, if that is all, I have the very remedy you need. In two hours' time all shall be well with you.'"[33]

The hunter left the cabin and returned with a sack of fat from a freshly killed bear that he rendered into a pint of oil. He told Everts to drink it.

Everts said, "It proved to be the needed remedy, and the next day, freed from pain, with appetite and digestion re-established, I felt that good food and plenty of it were only necessary for an early recovery."[34]

When Everts got his ability to eat back, he began to recover. Two days later, Baronett took him to the wagon that waited at the mouth of Yankee Jim Canyon. From there, he went to Bozeman and the care of friends for several days. Then he returned home to Helena, where he was greeted as a hero and feted with a banquet.

CHAPTER EIGHT
Geyserland and Home

WATER IN THE HOT SPRINGS NEAR THE EXPEDITION'S CAMP ROSE SILENTLY through the night and boiled over violently before daylight on the morning of September 17. The roar of the springs frightened Langford's saddle horse, and the animal bolted away. The horse ran close to a spring where the crust collapsed under the animal's weight, and he sank down to his belly. In the horse's struggle to safety, he cut his foot so badly that Langford decided to let him rest and ride his smaller packhorse—the one that had punched through the crust during the trip to Brown Mountain five days before. The hair had fallen off the packhorse's scalded leg, but otherwise he was fine.

The mood in the camp was gloomy. The party had held a conference the night before and decided to abandon the search for Truman Everts and rush home. Langford said, "We have discussed the situation from every point of view, and have tried to put ourselves in his place and have considered all the possibilities of fate that may befall him. Has he met death by accident, or may he be injured and unable to move, and be suffering the horrors of starvation and fever? Has he wandered aimlessly hither and thither until bereft of reason?"[1]

Langford's speculations about Everts were uncanny. The nearsighted former tax collector did indeed wander back and forth in search of help, suffer scalds, burns, and injuries, and eventually succumb to starvation-induced hallucinations. It would be weeks before he was found babbling incoherently.

Warren Gillette objected to the groups' decision to abandon Everts and volunteered to continue the search if someone else would go with him. When none of the civilians volunteered, Lieutenant Doane ordered two men from the Army escort to accompany Gillette. The explorers provided the trio with food from their dwindling supply and sent them on their way. The camp settled down after Gillette left to make one last attempt to find Everts. The rest of the party packed up and reluctantly started westward to search for the Grand Geysers on the Firehole River, one of the main objectives of the expedition.

They traveled six miles through open timber before encountering fallen pine, but the tangled deadfall was not as difficult to get through as it had been on the east side of the lake. Snow still covered the ground, and rain continued to fall. Packhorses got mired in mud, and the men had to free them, making travel slow.

About noon, the expedition finished a steep climb and crossed the Continental Divide from the Yellowstone drainage to the Snake River drainage. Looking southward, they saw what is now called Shoshone Lake. Some of the men thought the lake might be the headwater of the Firehole River and that following its outlet would lead to the Grand Geysers. But others pointed out there was no mountain ridge south of the lake, so it must be the headwater of the Snake River. The way south along the Snake looked easy, thus buoying the explorers' hopes that Everts might have made his way to settlements there by going in that direction.

The explorers headed west over the rugged mountains. They were confident they would find the Firehole River and could follow it to geyserland. In the afternoon, they crossed the Continental Divide again from the Snake River to the headwaters of the Madison. They camped on the Madison side near a spring of good water in a small open valley. Although there was still about five inches of snow on the ground, plenty of tall grass lay under it, allowing the horses to graze and regain strength after the sparse pickings they found near the hot springs at West Thumb.

The food supply was running out, so the men had a scant meal. Some were fatigued, and others depressed and still wondered what watershed they were on, but Langford wrote in his journal that evening, "I do not know of any day since we left home when I have been in better spirits. I am sure we are on the right course and feel no anxiety."[2]

The weather was bleak, and rain seemed imminent, but there wasn't anywhere big enough to pitch the large pavilion tent, so the men searched for dry spots under the trees where they could sleep. Langford found a dry spot where he fastened a ridgepole to the trees and built a wickiup with a thatched roof of overlapping pine boughs. He advised the others to build themselves shelters, but they ignored him.

At about 11:00 p.m., Cornelius Hedges finished his turn of guard duty and joined Langford in the wickiup. A deluge began about 3:00 a.m., and several members of the party sought shelter with them. Langford said,

"Hedges and I crawled out of our dry blankets, and sat upright, so as to make as much room as possible for the others, and we welcomed all our comrades to our dry shelter."[3]

Langford said General Washburn suffered from the cold and was "especially grateful for the protection from the storm, which continued until about 7 o'clock." Frail health was the main reason the distinguished Civil War general was in the West. He had decided not to seek reelection to the US House of Representatives and persuaded his old friend, President U. S. Grant, to appoint him surveyor general of Montana in hopes that life in the West would restore his vigor. It hadn't worked.

THE NEXT MORNING, THE MEN HUDDLED AROUND THEIR CAMPFIRE, TRYING to dry their rain-soaked clothes and to eat another scant meal in silence. Just as they were finishing breakfast, some wild animal rustled the brush and spooked the party's horses that were picketed nearby. Langford said, "In their violent plunging they pulled up the iron picket pins attached to their lariats, and dashed at a gallop directly through our camp, over the campfire, and upsetting and scattering hither and thither our cooking utensils. The iron picket pins flying through the air at the lariat ends narrowly missed several of our party, but became entangled with the only two sound packsaddles remaining of the entire number with which we started, and dashed them against the adjacent trees, tearing off the side pieces of the saddle trees, and rendering them useless."

It looked like the damage was beyond repair, but Langford dug into his sack of equipment and came up with nippers, a screwdriver, and two dozen screws and nails of various sizes. With the things from Langford's stash and some boards salvaged from empty canned-goods boxes, the packers managed to fix the damaged packsaddles and the explorers began traveling again.

Commenting on his companions' lack of supplies, Langford joked that the expedition would be known as the "Temperance Party." Only he and one other man had brought a flask of whiskey. He also mentioned things he alone had brought, such as waterproof boots and clothing.

In about two hours, the party struck a large stream running north. In his abbreviated journal notes, Hedges described the scene: "Saw columns of steam assuring us that we were on Fire Hole River—quite a large stream with great falls—continual cascade—followed river two miles or more, stopping at one mound raised by hot spring. Soon came in sight of great geyser."

Langford said, "In the clear sunlight, at no great distance, an immense volume of clear, sparkling water projected into the air to the height of one hundred and twenty-five feet."

"Geysers! Geysers!" somebody exclaimed, and everyone spurred their tired horses forward. The men had arrived at the Upper Geyser Basin.

Walter Trumbull described the basin this way: "It was nearly destitute of vegetation, but there were a few clumps of trees scattered through it, and in one place we found grass enough for our horses. The basin was chiefly on the west side of the river, but there was a narrow strip, with an average width of three hundred yards, on the east side, which was literally alive with geysers and steam-jets."

Langford was just as expansive: "Judge, then, of our astonishment on entering this basin, to see at no great distance before us an immense body of sparkling water, projected suddenly and with terrific force into the air to the height of over one hundred feet. We had found a real geyser. In the valley before us were a thousand hot springs of various sizes and character."

The geyser basin, two miles long and a mile wide, was mostly covered with a barren white powder, but the explorers found a place to camp where there was enough grass for their horses.

The men scattered to investigate the geysers and hot springs. Langford and Hedges took off their boots to ford the Firehole River. The current dashed over boulders, but they found a spot where the river bottom had a smooth rock surface that would allow them to cross. At the middle of the stream, Langford noticed his feet were getting hot. He recalled the tall tale of the mountain man Jim Bridger, who said he knew of a river where the water ran so fast that it made its bottom hot. Langford attributed the heat to a steam vent.

A LASTING LEGACY OF THE WASHBURN EXPEDITION WAS THE NAMES THE men gave to the largest geysers in the Upper Basin. Earlier visitors to the basin had probably conjured fanciful names for the things they had seen, but those names didn't stick. Langford commented, "We gave such names to those of the geysers we saw in action as we think will best illustrate their peculiarities."

Grotto Geyser is one of the features in the Upper Geyser Basin that still bears the name given to it by the Washburn Expedition.
NATIONAL PARK SERVICE

General Washburn published geyser names and descriptions in the *Helena Daily Herald* just a few days after the expedition returned to civilization. Also important were N. P. Langford's descriptions that were published a few months later in *Scribner's Monthly*. Early park visitors often took copies of Langford's *Scribner's* article to identify the objects they saw. Soon, park guidebooks that used Washburn Expedition names for the geysers became available.

Old Faithful was the geyser the explorers saw when they first arrived at the Upper Basin, and General Washburn soon noted that it played regularly and suggested the name. Walter Trumbull published expansive descriptions of the geysers in the May-June 1871 issue of *Overland Monthly*. He wrote, "Old Faithful was the first geyser we saw throwing up a column of water. It was named on account of its almost constant action. It did not intermit for more than an hour at any time during our stay. It had a vent five feet by three, and projected a solid column of water to a height of eighty or ninety feet."

Old Faithful was the first geyser the Washburn Expedition saw in the Upper Geyser Basin. General Washburn named it for its regular and frequent eruptions.

The party camped across the basin from a family of cone geysers—the Lion, the Lioness, the Big Cub, and the Little Cub—that are connected underground. Of these, the Lion is the largest and spouts up to ninety feet and makes a roaring sound that reminded the explorers of a lion.

From their camp, the explorers scattered across the basin, observing and naming geysers and springs. The largest geyser cone in the basin is the Castle, which stands forty feet tall. Trumbull said, "The Castle was the largest cone, or mass of incrustations, in the basin. For a hundred yards around, the ground, flooded with subsilica, of glittering whiteness, sloped gradually up to the cone, which itself rose thirty feet, nearly perpendicular. It was quite rugged and efflorescent, and on its outer sides had a number of benches, sufficiently wide for a man to stand upon. These enabled us to climb up and look into its crater, which was irregular in shape, and about seven feet, the longest way, by five feet, the shortest. The outside of the mound was nearly round, and not less than thirty feet through at its base."

Down the river a few hundred yards from the Castle, the men found a cone standing twelve feet tall. It had a piece knocked out of one side where the men could peer down the crater into a tube six feet in diameter. This giant threw a six-foot column of water a hundred feet up. Doane said, "When it played, it doubled the size of the Firehole River." This huge amount of water earned the geyser its name, "the Giant."

Two hundred yards farther, they found a peculiar cone pocked with holes large enough for a man to crawl into—and some of the men did. They promptly dubbed it the Grotto. Trumbull said the Grotto had two craters "connected by a ridge or neck or incrustations two feet high. The larger mound of incrustations was about ten feet high, and twenty feet through at the base. The smaller mound was not more than five feet high, and shaped like a haycock, with a portion of the top knocked off." He added that the larger crater was "about five feet in diameter, and that the smaller, not more than three feet." He said when Grotto's craters played, "a solid stream was thrown up more than sixty feet."

The men crossed the river from the Grotto and found another geyser. That one, Trumbull said, was named "the Fantail geyser from the fact that it discharged two streams from its vent which spread out very much like a fan."

Across the river from the expedition's camp was a geyser on a hill made of deposits from the water it expelled. They called it "the Giantess." Trumbull said, "When quiet, it was a clear, beautiful pool, caught in a subsilica urn, or vase, with a hollow, bottomless stem, through which the steam came bubbling, just like the effervescence of champagne from the bottom of a long, hollow-necked glass." When it erupted, he said, the Giantess "became a fountain with five jets, shooting the spray to a height of two hundred feet." The men saw the Giantess play at sunset when "the last rays of light gave prismatic tints to the glistening drops," and "the boiling water became a golden fleece lit up by wreaths of rainbows." The Giantess threw a column of water twenty feet in diameter to a height of ninety feet and individual jets up to 250 feet. Though inferior to "the Giant, in immensity of volume and perhaps in grandeur, the Giantess was by far the most beautiful sight we saw in the geyser basin," Trumbull said.

Another geyser on the same side of the river as the Giantess caught the explorers by surprise. General Washburn described it as "a small hot spring that had apparently built itself up about three feet." This cone reminded the men of an old-fashioned rope beehive, and that's what they named it, "the Beehive." General Washburn said, "While we were eating breakfast, this spring, without any warning threw, as if it were a nozzle of an enormous steam engine, a stream of water into the air two-hundred and nineteen feet."

THE MEN WERE FASCINATED WITH THE GEYSERS AND WOULD HAVE STAYED longer to investigate them, but they were acutely aware of their diminishing supplies, so they decided to move on. They had been in the Upper Geyser Basin less than two days.

The packers started their slow-moving train at about 9:30 on the morning of September 18, but the other explorers remained behind, hoping to see the Giantess Geyser erupt one more time. The Giantess just teased them with its water repeatedly rising about ten feet in its well and then falling back, so they moved on.

Hedges wanted to supplement the party's diminished food supply by fishing, but he was disappointed to find there were no fish in the Firehole River. Early travelers attributed the barren waters to heat and chemicals from the geothermal features, but scientists later concluded that was wrong. Actually, massive lava flows millions of years before had formed waterfalls and cascades that kept fish from migrating upstream, so they couldn't repopulate the river after the ice age glaciers melted.

The explorers headed north on the east bank of the Firehole River, sometimes through an open valley and other times through fallen timber. After about eight miles, they came to the Midway Geyser basin, where they stopped briefly to admire hot springs so large that the men called them "hot lakes."

Langford described the largest, now called Grand Prismatic Spring, this way: "Out near the center of the lake the water boils up a few feet, but without any especial violent action. The lake has no well-defined outlet, but overflows on many sides, the water flowing down the slopes of the incrusted mound about one-quarter of an inch deep." Langford walked around it, counting his paces, and concluded it was 450 yards in diameter.

Another "hot lake" the explorers examined was the mouth of the Excelsior Geyser, which is almost as large as Grand Prismatic Spring. They didn't know it was a geyser because it didn't erupt when they were there. The Excelsior's first observed eruption was in 1880, when it sent a column of water three hundred feet wide three hundred feet into the air, which made it by far the largest geyser in the world. The Excelsior is now dormant.

Langford said a flock of ducks sailed over the lake as if they planned to land, then rose into the air, all except one. That one "came down into the water, and his frantic efforts to rise again were futile, and with one or two loud squawks of distress, which were responded to by his mates who had escaped, he was in a moment 'a dead duck.'"

Always eager to take a dig at Jake Smith, Langford said the businessman collected his first specimen at these giant springs, an unusual piece of tufa. The specimen shattered when Smith's horse stumbled and he dropped it. Langford said Smith's outburst was "at variance with his own Bible instruction, and he denounced as worthless all specimens."

When the party came to the Lower Geyser Basin, they saw a large geyser, probably the Great Fountain, playing in the distance, and a number of columns of steam rising, but they didn't stop to investigate. They didn't want to cross the swampy ground between their trail and the area. Besides, their supplies were critically low, and they were rushing on. They had planned for a twenty-five-day trip, had already been gone thirty days, and had left supplies behind for Everts to find. The fish Cornelius Hedges had caught and dried at Yellowstone Lake were helping to pull them through, but they needed to get to civilization.

As they rode along, Ben Stickney complained that the larder was running out of coffee and sugar, so Langford pulled a block of maple sugar from his stash and shared it with the others.

Stickney told Langford, "You always seem to have another card up your sleeve when an emergency arises." In his book, Langford used the card remark to take another dig at Jake Smith, saying it reminded him of how the man played poker.

AFTER TRAVELING EIGHTEEN MILES FROM THE UPPER GEYSER BASIN, THE party camped where the Gibbon River joined the Firehole River to form the Madison. According to Langford, it was here that members of the expedition first discussed the idea of setting aside the area they had just seen as a national park. Langford said the men were sitting around their campfire when someone suggested that staking claims around Yellowstone Falls and the Upper Geyser Basin would be profitable. According to Langford, Cornelius Hedges objected and said, "There ought to be no private ownership of any portion of the region, but that the whole of it ought to be set apart as a great national park."[4]

Langford said Hedges's suggestion "met with an instantaneous and favorable response from all—except one—of the members of our party."[5] He added that the idea dominated the group's discussions the next day.

There is no mention of preserving the area as a park in the diaries of other members of the expedition, including Hedges. This omission has led historians to doubt that it ever happened.[6] Despite doubts about the veracity of the Madison campfire story, it became a cornerstone of Yellowstone Park lore. In 1906, just one year after Langford's book was published, the Yellowstone photographer Jack Haynes included a version of it in his famous *Haynes Guide* that he sold to thousands of park visitors. Updated versions of the guide were published until 1962 and helped secure Langford's reputation as a prime force in establishing the park.

It's not surprising that Haynes, a major park concessionaire, would promote the Madison campfire story, which offers altruistic motives for founding the park and obscured its origins in the moneymaking schemes of people planning railroads and hotels. The story also made a convenient appeal for park officials seeking funding and public support. Versions of it were included in official publications, anniversary celebrations, and ranger talks. The Park

In 1960 reenactors posed at the site of the Washburn Expedition's camp near the confluence of the Firehole and Gibbon Rivers. N. P. Langford said the idea of creating a national park was born there.
NATIONAL PARK SERVICE

Service even put up signs near the confluence of the Firehole and Gibbon Rivers to commemorate the story.

ON SEPTEMBER 20, THE MORNING AFTER THE PURPORTED DISCUSSION about establishing a national park, camp was broken about nine o'clock. Just below camp, they had to ford the Madison River twice before entering a narrow canyon enclosed by bare rock walls that stood straight up for a thousand feet. They tried to travel by the river on a grassy, narrow shelf, but often they encountered rock debris and boulders that forced them to ride in the shallow river.

After traveling twelve miles through the canyon through what Doane called the "grandest vistas of volcanic mountain scenery,"[7] the men came to a plateau that sloped to the west. They traveled through heavy timber until they came to two tall hills in the middle of the valley. Lieutenant Doane and Langford climbed the highest hill and surveyed the area. Doane said it formed a circle twenty miles across. The Madison River ran through the center of the valley, where it was surrounded by pine trees because the elevation was too high for cottonwoods. Doane commented that the party should have skirted the forested area by the river by traveling on open land next to the mountains.

As they rode along, Jake Smith asked Langford if he expected readers of his diary to believe what he had written. According to Langford, Smith said he didn't keep a diary because he didn't think people would believe the things he saw. Smith said he didn't mind being called a liar by his friends, but he would not allow strangers the privilege. Langford couldn't resist another dig at Smith. In his journal, Langford wrote, "This ambiguous remark indicates that Jake has more wit and philosophy than I have given him the credit of possessing."

The expedition camped that night near where a large stream ran into the Madison. Although they were approaching civilization, they still posted guards.

Hauser and Stickney had ridden ahead of the rest of the group most of the day. Shortly after they came out of the canyon, they met two men who seemed alarmed to see them. The men were walking beside horses that carried a supply of provisions. Hauser told the men they would soon meet a larger group coming down the canyon, but the men disappeared into the timber before the main group arrived.

Doane noted, "This district has a bad reputation, as being a place of rendezvous for the bands of horse-thieves and road agents which infest the Territory." He said the area had dense forests to hide in and ample grazing for stolen horses, "rendering it a pleasant and secure retreat for lawless men."[8]

After a long day traveling thirty miles, the men camped in a deep, wooded ravine near a clear, beautiful creek and soon had a rousing campfire.

On September 22, just one month after leaving Fort Ellis, the expedition reached civilization in the form of a ranch on the Madison River. Young Walter Trumbull said of this arrival: "It was a little strange to feel that we were again within the pale of civilization. During our month's absence, we had seen so much that was new and strange that it seemed more like a year. Every one felt funny; and we looked at each other and laughed in a silly way, as one small boy does, when, on entering church or any other place where he ought to keep quiet, he catches the eye of another small-boy acquaintance. There was a pleasure in getting home; and all felt curious to hear the newspapers, old and new, were alike seized, and devoured with wonderful avidity."

Langford estimated the distance to Virginia City at thirty miles and decided to rush there the next morning. He left at dawn with Johnny, one of the African-American cooks. Apparently he hoped to hear word of Truman Everts. Probably he also wanted to be the first man to tell Montana newspapers about the party's return from their visit to Wonderland.

CHAPTER NINE
Persuading the World

As soon as the Washburn Expedition got safely back to settled parts of Montana, N. P. Langford began working to get the area he had just seen reserved as a park. The day after the purported campfire story, September 21, the Washburn Expedition exited the middle canyon of the Madison River and camped by the banks of a small stream. The next morning, Langford estimated the distance to Virginia City and decided he could get there by nightfall. He packed a lunch and rushed ahead of his companions. Langford got to town at about 9:00 p.m., two hours after the telegraph office closed, so he had to wait until the next morning to send a telegram. He must have done that first thing, because the *Helena Daily Herald* published news of the Washburn party's return and the loss of Truman Everts in its September 23 issue, reports that were based on Langford's telegrams. The newspaper published a fuller account on September 24 based on notes he provided. Thus, Langford succeeding in getting credit for announcing the return of the Washburn Expedition.

The *Helena Herald* published the first account written by a member of the expedition, General Washburn, in two installments on September 27–28. Washburn provided a travelogue that described the sights he had seen in a clear, readable style. He made his most enduring contribution by naming the principal geysers of the Upper Basin and describing them in enough detail that subsequent travelers could recognize them. The names stuck.

The newspaper's own correspondent, Cornelius Hedges, said he had pressing matters in his law practice and thus didn't provide an account until two weeks later. Hedges then began a series of four articles on October 7. A statement in Hedges's last installment, which was published on November 9, is noteworthy. In it, Hedges advocated that "the Territorial lines be so readjusted that Montana should embrace all that lake region west of the Wind River Range, a manner in which we hope our citizens will soon move

to accomplish, as well as to secure its future appropriation to the public use."
Apparently, he wanted the area turned over to Montana so it could become a
park like Yosemite, which had been granted to California in 1864.

It was common practice at the time for newspapers to reprint each other's articles. News of the Washburn Expedition spread across the country.

While N. P. Langford's companions wrote for Montana newspapers,
he aimed for a national audience. He published a two-part series about the
Washburn Expedition in *Scribner's Monthly* that appeared in the May and
June 1871 issues of the magazine. *Scribner's* was so popular that newspapers
frequently announced the content of upcoming issues, thus amplifying Langford's role in the Washburn Expedition.

In his articles, Langford described the things he had seen as "the most
stupendous on the continent" and put in a plug for the Northern Pacific Railroad. "When the railroad is completed," he predicted, "thousands of tourists will come to behold with their own eyes the wonders here described."[1]
Thomas Moran provided fanciful illustrations for the article, apparently based
on Langford's descriptions. Moran wouldn't actually see the wonders of the
Yellowstone until a year later, when he accompanied the Hayden Expedition,
the first federally funded exploration of the area. Moran gained fame for his
Yellowstone paintings, including the giant seven-by-twelve-foot *Grand Canyon of the Yellowstone*, which is now on display at the Smithsonian Institution.

Walter Trumbull published an account of the Washburn Expedition at
the same time as Langford. It appeared in the May–June 1871 issue of the
less-prestigious *Overland Monthly*, a San Francisco–based magazine with
a national circulation. Trumbull provided a day-by-day description of the
group's travels and the sights the explorers saw. "During our month's absence,
we had seen so much that was new and strange that it seemed more like a
year,"[2] he wrote. He said the area would not be good for agriculture except
possibly for sheep raising, but the "portion of America will be more popular
as a watering-place or summer resort than that which we had the pleasure of
viewing, in all the glory and grandeur of its primeval solitude."

When Truman Everts, the man who strayed away from the Washburn
Expedition, was found alive on October 21, newspapers were eager to publish
his amazing survival story, and people all over America became interested in
it. *Scribner's Monthly* accommodated that interest and published his "Thirty-
Seven Days of Peril" in its November 1871 issue. Everts told about dramatic

incidents such as being treed by a mountain lion and fashioning a fishhook from the wire rim of his broken glasses. He also described holding conversations with his stomach and legs and being guided by a ghostly apparition—visions that probably resulted from hallucinations brought on by starvation. Everts's engaging tale captured public imagination and is credited with helping to get the US Congress to create Yellowstone National Park.

Langford wanted to generate more attention than his articles provided and went to work on notes for public lectures. By November 11, he had a manuscript about thirteen thousand words long.[3] Langford gave his lectures twice in Montana, in Helena on November 18 and in Virginia City on November 22.

Early in 1872, he made presentations to much fanfare in the East. James G. Blaine, the Speaker of the US House of Representatives, introduced Langford at his lecture at Lincoln Hall in Washington, DC, on January 19. The lecture generated newspaper coverage and, perhaps more important, the head of the US Geological Survey, Ferdinand Vandiveer Hayden, was in the audience. A few months later, Hayden would lead the first government-sponsored exploration of the area that became Yellowstone National Park.

Langford reprised his lecture at New York City's Cooper Union on January 21. He later said that he proposed establishing a national park during his lectures, but newspaper accounts don't corroborate that, and the idea isn't mentioned in his notes.[4] They do, however, document that a thrust of Langford's lecture was to popularize the Northern Pacific Railroad route that promoters hoped would approach the area by the mid-1870s, but the Financial Panic of 1873 stalled track building. The railroad didn't arrive there until 1883.

LANGFORD'S LECTURES AND OTHER PUBLICITY ABOUT THE WASHBURN Expedition, along with lobbying from the Northern Pacific Railroad, prompted the US Congress to allocate $40,000 for exploration of the area at the headwaters of the Yellowstone and Madison Rivers. In the spring of 1871, even before money for the new fiscal year became available, Ferdinand Vandiveer Hayden began organizing an expedition.

The secretary of the interior instructed Hayden "to secure as much information as possible, both scientific and practical, you will give your attention to the geological, mineralogical, zoological, botanical, and agricultural

Ferdinand Vandiveer Hayden led the first government survey of the head-waters of the Yellowstone and Madison Rivers. He recommended the area be set aside as a national park.

NATIONAL PARK SERVICE, PHOTO BY WILLIAM HENRY JACKSON, 1871

resources of the country. You will collect as ample material as possible for the illustration of your final reports, such as sketches, sections, photographs, etc."[5]

This was an enormous charge, but Hayden managed to stretch his resources. He received permission to draw supplies from western Army posts, and the Union Pacific and Central Pacific railroads provided shipping and transportation.

While Hayden assembled his men and supplies at Ogden, Utah, he received a letter from Captain John W. Barlow, chief engineer of the Army's Missouri Division. Barlow said General Philip Sheridan had ordered him to "join your party previous to its entering the 'Great Basin.'"[6] About the same time, Hayden received a letter from a Northern Pacific Railroad official stating that the artist Thomas Moran wanted to join the expedition. Moran's paintings, along with the pioneering outdoor photographs by William Henry Jackson, provided visual documentation of the area and helped persuade the US Congress to establish Yellowstone Park. Pictures taken by a photographer with Captain Barlow's party were burned in the Chicago Fire of October 1871.

The Hayden and Barlow teams coordinated their efforts with the Army focused on land surveys, while the civilians, following directions from the secretary of the interior, focused on the resources of the country.

Hayden took his charge of collecting samples seriously, and his men's efforts at gathering insect specimens caused locals to derisively label them "bug hunters." The two teams combined totaled more than fifty men, and they spent more than a month gathering information and specimens such as "geyser eggs," the balls of silica found in geothermal features. They sent dozens of pack mules loaded with objects they had collected for shipment to the Smithsonian Institution.

Lieutenant Gustavus Doane wanted to head the Army escort for Hayden's party as he had for the Washburn Expedition, but he was in Saint Paul, Minnesota, testifying in a court-martial when the group left Fort Ellis. He returned to the West and took over command of the escort nearly a month after Hayden entered the park area.

Doane thought Hayden's work would eclipse his own accomplishments on the Washburn Expedition the year before. He feared Hayden's reports might not even mention them. That's not surprising. Doane's own reports hadn't mentioned the accomplishments of the Folsom-Cook-Peterson party

The *Annie* was the first boat to sail Yellowstone Lake. The Hayden Expedition
of 1871 used her to map the shoreline and take depth soundings.
NATIONAL PARK SERVICE, PHOTO BY WILLIAM HENRY JACKSON, 1871

the year before his trip to the park area. Doane caught up with the Hayden
party at Yellowstone Lake, where he discovered they had launched the *Annie*,
the lake's first sailboat, to map the shoreline and take soundings of its depths.
Doane also found that Hayden and his men had mapped and named every
geyser and spring they could find.

NEWSPAPERS REPORTED THE PROGRESS OF THE HAYDEN EXPEDITION AS IT
passed cities and towns along the railroad tracks across the country and then
headed north. They even managed to get a few reports from travelers and
couriers while the expedition was in the park area.

Coverage intensified when members of the Hayden Party got back to
civilization. On September 7, the *Helena Daily Herald* reported that "Gentlemen who have just returned from the volcanic region of the Yellowstone
country report that the statements heretofore made regarding the wonders
there exhibited are in no ways exaggerated." The *Herald* added: "We predict
that in five years the Valley of the Yellowstone will have become a resort for

pleasure-seekers of all lands. No portion of the world so far known presents the attractions approaching this strange region."[7]

By October, members of the Hayden Expedition had dispersed to cities across the nation, and newspapers eagerly sought them out as sources for accounts of what they had seen. The men usually provided detailed descriptions and extolled the virtues of the area.

On October 4, 1871, the *Chicago Tribune* published a letter from its own correspondent that described what he saw while accompanying the Hayden Expedition. He described his entire tour from its departure from Bozeman until it returned to the settlements along the Madison and Jefferson Rivers. He described the major sights in the order he encountered them. Among them were what he called "white mountain," which was later named Mammoth Hot Springs. He described it as "a series of terraces the whole looking like some vast frozen cascade." He added: "The deposit in some places is fashioned into basins with scalloped edges, some of which are of a pure white

The Hayden Expedition gathered on the bank of Yellowstone Lake for a photo. They assessed the geological and biological resources of the area and named mountains, streams, and lakes.
NATIONAL PARK SERVICE, PHOTO BY WILLIAM HENRY JACKSON, 1871

color. Others are tinted with pink, red, and orange giving them the most pleasing appearance." He lauded other features—Yellowstone Falls and Lake, and the geysers—with equally high praise. He added: "When the Northern Pacific Railroad runs through this country, as no doubt it shortly will, this will become one of the places of resort for tourists, as it is one of the greatest curiosities on the continent."

The *New York Herald* of October 30, 1871, reprinted an article from the *Boston Advertiser* that noted Hayden had returned to that city. Hayden told the *Advertiser* about the exploration of Yellowstone Lake and described a geyser that "throws a column of hot water eight feet in diameter to a height of two hundred feet at regular intervals of thirty-two hours."

The *Chicago Tribune* of September 21, 1871, reprinted an article from the *Sacramento Bee* based on an interview with a "Mr. Adams," who was a botanist on the Hayden Expedition. Adams praised the Yellowstone Falls, "which rivals Niagara in beauty," and said, "Mud Geysers were more curious than beautiful."

AFTER HAYDEN FINISHED HIS FIELDWORK EARLY IN OCTOBER, HE RETURNED to Washington, DC. By the end of the month, he had received a letter from an official of the Northern Pacific Railroad endorsing the idea that Congress should reserve the great geyser basin as a public park and noting that he had included the idea in his official report. Hayden, in turn, endorsed that.

Apparently, the Northern Pacific immediately recruited N. P. Langford, who was in Montana, to promote the park. The Bozeman *Avant Courier* reported on November 9 that Langford "yesterday received a dispatch from Gov. Marshall of Minnesota to return immediately to Minnesota as important business concerning the Northern Pacific Railroad awaited him." That evening, Langford was on the stagecoach to Utah so he could take the train back east.

By the end of December 1871, articles that credited Langford with organizing the lobbying effort to establish Yellowstone Park began appearing across the nation. In these articles, Langford somehow managed not only to upstage Hayden as the head of the effort but also to get himself called the leader of the Washburn Expedition. One from the *New Orleans Republican* of December 22, 1871, was typical. It said: "Hon. N. P. Langford, of Montana, the leader of the famous Yellowstone expedition last year, is now in

Washington and in connection with Professor Hayden, who had charge of the governmental expedition of this year, is engaged in promoting the project of declaring all that district, including the canyon of the Yellowstone, the hot springs and geysers a governmental reservation, for the purpose of holding it forever as a national park."

ON DECEMBER 18, 1871, A BILL DRAFTED BY MONTANA TERRITORIAL DELegate William H. Clagett was submitted to the US Congress. Some marveled that Clagett, who had been in office only two weeks, could write such a well-crafted bill. Apparently, he modeled it after the one that reserved the Yosemite Valley as a park. The largest difference was the Yosemite grant provided that area to the State of California for administration, while Clagett's bill put Yellowstone under the US Department of the Interior. As a courtesy, Clagett let US senator Samuel Clarke Pomeroy introduce the bill first in the Senate, then he introduced it to the House of Representatives later that same morning.

In February, Seth Bullock, who would later be among Yellowstone Park's first tourists, wrote what was called a "memorial" for the Montana legislature, requesting that the northeast corner of Wyoming be annexed to Montana. Bullock argued that massive mountain ranges made access to the park area nearly impossible from Wyoming, that rivers originating in the area all flowed through Montana, and residents of Montana were responsible for exploring it. The memorial also requested that the area be set aside "for all time to come as a great National Park."[8]

Hayden arranged for artifacts gathered on his 1871 survey to be displayed in the Capitol Rotunda along with selected photographs by William Henry Jackson and watercolor sketches by Thomas Moran.[9] Copies of *Scribner's* magazine containing Langford's "Wonders of Yellowstone" article, along with Lieutenant Gustavus Doane's official report of the Washburn Expedition, were given to all senators and congressmen.

In describing the efforts of Langford and himself, Delegate Clagett later recalled that "I believe there was not a single member of Congress in either house who was not fully posted by one or another of us in personal interviews."[10] Clagett was likely exaggerating when he said, "Langford and I probably did two-thirds, if not three-fourths of all the work connected with its passage,"[11] but doubtless the men's efforts were important.[12]

On January 22, Senator Pomeroy reported the bill out of the Committee on Public Lands and recommended its passage, but he withdrew when there was a procedural objection. The Senate considered the bill again on September 30. Several senators spoke in favor of it, including Lyman Trumbull of Illinois, the father of Walter Trumbull, the youngest member of the Washburn Expedition.

Only Senator Cornelius Cole of California objected to the bill. Cole argued that the law was unnecessary because "the natural curiosities there cannot be interfered by anything that man can do. The geysers will remain, no matter where the ownership of the land may be."[13] Cole said that settlers should be allowed to make claims in the area and that there was an abundance of public park ground in the Rocky Mountains. Senator Trumbull countered that the law could be repealed later if it proved to be in anybody's way, and it passed on a voice vote.

After the US Senate passed Clagett's bill, it languished in the House of Representatives, but there was a flurry of publications supporting it. The *Helena Daily Herald* of February 1, 1872, noted that the bill had passed the Senate and said the park idea was conceived "by a party of gentlemen from this city, who visited this region of wonders in the summer of 1869 and gave to the world the first reliable reports concerning its marvels of wealth of natural curiosities, the project has gained ground with surprising rapidity." The paper was referring to the exploration by David Folsom, Charles Cook, and William Peterson. Of course others, including Montana territorial governor Thomas Francis Meagher, had suggested reserving the area.

The newspaper continued, "In letters of Mr. Hedges, first published in the *Herald*, the lectures of Mr. Langford, the articles of Mr. Trumbull, and later still, the story of peril and adventure of Mr. Everts, all of the same party, were widely circulated by the press of the country, and not merely excited a passing curiosity, but created a living general interest that has since received strength and larger proportions by the publication of Lieutenant Doane's official report to the war department of the same expedition; followed, as that was, by the expedition of Professor Hayden during the last summer, under the patronage of the Smithsonian Institution, with its fully appointed corps of scientific gentlemen and distinguished artists, whose reports have more than confirmed all descriptions of the Washburn Party."

After this Herculean sentence, the *Herald* added, "Without a doubt the Northern Pacific Railroad will have a branch track penetrating this Plutonian region, and few seasons will pass before excursion trains will daily be sweeping into this great park thousands of the curious from all parts of the world."

Of course there was some opposition to the bill that focused on the rights of private citizens to settle in the park. James McCartney and his partner, Harry Horr, had built their cabin near Mammoth Hot Springs in the summer of 1871. That was before Yellowstone Park was established, and squatters' rights were generally recognized at the time. McCartney and Horr circulated a petition in hopes of getting an exception for their property written into the bill, but that never happened.

The Helena *Rocky Mountain Weekly Gazette* of February 18, 1872, supported the settlers and said, "We regard the project with little favor, unless Congress will go still further and make appropriations to open carriage roads and hostels in the reserved district, so that ordinary humanity can get to it without having to ride the 'hurricane deck' of a mule." The *Gazette* also noted "already private enterprise was taking measures to render the country accessible" and said that under the provisions of the bill "all these private enterprises will cease." The newspaper opposed the bill because it would affect development of the park area and "remand it into perpetual solitude, by shutting out private enterprise and by preventing individual energy from opening the country to the general traveling public."[14]

The bill to create Yellowstone Park finally came up in ordinary business on February 27. After the bill was read that day, Representative Henry L. Dawes of Massachusetts rose to support it. Dawes noted that the bill followed the precedent set when the government granted the Yosemite Valley to California for a park, except that it kept the Yellowstone area under federal control. He added that the proposed area's elevation, at seven thousand feet above sea level, meant it could never be settled for agriculture.

Dawes continued that the area "contained the most sublime scenery in the United States" and "the most wonderful geysers found in the country."[15] For some reason, Dawes did not go as far as Ferdinand Hayden had in his official reports on his survey of the park, which was available to the House. Hayden noted that the area lacked mineral wealth and that the geysers were by far the largest in the world.[16]

After Dawes responded to a question about the effect of the law on Indian treaties and settlement of the land, the House passed the bill by a vote of 115 to 65, with 60 not voting.

President Ulysses S. Grant signed the bill into law on March 1, 1872. By then, N. P. Langford had gotten himself credit for being the leader of the Washburn Expedition that brought the wonders of Yellowstone Park to widespread attention and as a principal mover of the effort to establish it. He became the obvious candidate to become the superintendent of the new 3,468-square-mile park.

CHAPTER TEN

Superintendent Langford

N. P. Langford was named the first superintendent of Yellowstone National Park. Philetus Norris was also considered for the job, but he withdrew when he found out no salary or budget had been allocated to manage the 3,468-square-mile wonderland. To support himself, Langford took a position as federal bank examiner for the Northwest United States. The job required him to travel a lot, and he visited the park only twice during his five-year tenure as superintendent. The first time was to force Matthew McGuirk to leave a resort near Mammoth Hot Springs after the park was declared off-limits to settlers, and the second time was to tour the park with the Hayden Expedition of 1872.

The US Congress probably intended for the park to raise its own revenue by charging for concessions, but Langford didn't issue any. He said he didn't approve concessions to keep profiteers from gaining a toehold in the park, but some historians say he was stalling so his friends at the Northern Pacific Railroad could get the lucrative licenses.[1]

Langford also said he rebuffed efforts by his friends in the US Congress for a salary because "I feared that some successful applicant for such a salaried position, giving little thought to the matter, would approve the applications for leases; and that as long as I could prevent the granting of any exclusive concessions I would be willing to serve as superintendent without compensation."[2]

Superintendent Langford received a steady stream of requests from private citizens to develop roads and hotels in the park, but he always turned them down. "It was apparent from an examination of these applications that the purpose of the applicants was to enclose with fences their holdings and charge visitors an admission fee," he said. "To have permitted them would have defeated the purpose of the act of dedication."[3]

Nathaniel Pitt Langford was the "spark plug" behind the Washburn Expedition and one of its main chroniclers. He was the first superintendent of Yellowstone Park.

NATIONAL PARK SERVICE, PHOTO BY WILLIAM HENRY JACKSON, 1871

Langford's high-minded rationale for denying applications has been called into question. In fact, eminent Yellowstone historian Aubrey Haines said, "He was probably stalling in the hope that the Northern Pacific Railroad would resume westward construction and become a contender."[4] The railroad was stalled by an economic downturn at the time, but eventually it became a major force in Yellowstone Park hotels and concessions, as well as by hauling tourists to the park.

Langford has his defenders, who note that he repeatedly wrote to Secretary of the Interior Columbus Delano to ask for money to improve the park.[5] Langford's requests, first for $150,000 and later for $100,000, went unanswered. His letters, his defenders say, were impassioned. He asked for money to protect the "Temple of the Living God." The defenders add that waiting for the railroad made no sense because the Northern Pacific's plan to push the second transcontinental railroad across Montana failed in a national economic collapse in 1873, shortly after Langford's term as park superintendent began.

It's impossible to ascertain Langford's motives, but after the Northern Pacific reorganized in 1877 and completed its transcontinental route in 1883, it immediately began building a spur from Livingston, Montana, to Yellowstone Park. Before long, the railroad organized subsidiaries that obtained lucrative concessions for hotels and a transportation company in the park.

Langford's passive approach to running Yellowstone Park created an exceptional period for travel there. The park remained a pristine wilderness that was not regulated or patrolled. Tourists could go anywhere they wanted. They could bathe in the pools at Mammoth Hot Springs. They could peer down the throat of Old Faithful's cone or climb on the formation at Castle Geyser. They could hunt the abundant big game or catch the fish that teemed in the rivers and lakes.

Publicity generated by the Washburn and Hayden Expeditions created nationwide—even worldwide—interest in seeing the wonders of the park, but it was difficult to visit there. Visitors from afar usually took the Union Pacific Railroad's transcontinental line to Utah, then came north on horseback or by stagecoach. Tourists also could take a steamboat up the Missouri to Fort Benton, Montana, and proceed by horse from there. In either case, the trip was so expensive and arduous that few people made the effort.

Of course by 1872, there were many settlements nearby, so adventurous pioneers could visit the park if they had time and transportation. But even for them, a trip to the park meant difficult travel. Rough roads led only as far as the edges of the park, to Mammoth Hot Springs on the north side and the Lower Geyser Basin on the west. Early tourists had to travel by horseback to see the Upper Geyser Basin, Yellowstone Lake, the Upper and Lower Falls, and the Grand Canyon. Travel on horseback was slow, and people tended to spend ample time at major sights. For example, tourists might spend a full week camped at the Upper Geyser Basin and hoping to see *all* of the geysers play.

There were only a few dozen tourists in the park at any given time, so few that when parties encountered each other, they usually stopped to exchange greetings and information. It must have been a marvelous time in the park when territorial merchants and ranchers could mix with European aristocracy, American dignitaries, and Army generals.

Even before Yellowstone Park was officially established, tourists began visiting the area. In the summer of 1871, Rossiter Raymond, the US commissioner of mines, was in Virginia City, Montana, on other business when he decided to organize a group for a tour. Raymond hired Gilman Sawtell, the homesteader and fish harvester from Henrys Lake, Idaho, as his guide. The job earned Sawtell credit for being Yellowstone's first paid tour guide.

Of course nobody had published any guidebooks back then, so Raymond and his companions took copies of N. P. Langford's descriptions of Wonderland in *Scribner's Monthly* with them. Langford's account was highly readable, but it proved to be an inadequate travel guide.[6]

Langford's article provided detailed descriptions of the Upper Geyser Basin, but when he went to Wonderland with the Washburn Expedition, they rushed past the Lower Geyser Basin and didn't explore it because their supplies were running out. Unlike the Washburn Expedition, Raymond's party approached the park from the west, so their first encounter with geysers was at the Lower Geyser Basin. They spent long hours trying to fit what they were seeing to Langford's descriptions. Raymond said, "Since, the largest eruptions we observed did not exceed forty-five feet in height, we set down his account as hugely overdrawn, and were deeply disgusted at the depravity of travelers."[7]

Sawtell commented, "If it were not for that there article in that there magazine, these yer springs would be considered a big thing, after all, and perhaps it was just as well to let the magazine go to thunder, and enjoy the scenery."[8]

Raymond's group has been called "Yellowstone's First Tourists."[9] But if "tourists" means people who travel for the sole purpose of seeing the sights and not to trap, prospect, or explore, that title probably belongs to Warren Angus Ferris, who was a clerk of the American Fur Company. Ferris heard trappers telling tales of boiling fountains hundreds of feet high at a mountain man rendezvous in 1833 and decided to see them for himself the next year. Thus, he became the first person to visit the area solely to see the wonders there.

But unlike Ferris, Raymond's group saw a long list of sights, including the Upper and Lower Geyser Basins, Yellowstone Lake, and the Upper and Lower Yellowstone Falls. Their adventures were colorfully chronicled by Calvin Clawson in a four-part series published in the *New Northwest*, a Deer Lodge, Montana, newspaper.[10] Clawson not only describes the sights the party encountered but also speculates on such things as using the finely ground minerals found in the geyser basins for ladies' cosmetics and embalming bodies in the calcium-laden waters. Clawson also describes the antics of men out for an enjoyable adventure. Like groups everywhere, they sometimes entertained themselves with strange contests—like seeing who could get "First Blood" by shooting a bald eagle.

PRESIDENT ULYSSES S. GRANT SIGNED THE BILL THAT CREATED YELLOWstone Park on March 1, 1872, and tourists began arriving there that summer. Many of the earliest tourists were parties of two or three young men who traveled on horseback. They usually brought a single packhorse with them to carry equipment and food and planned to supplement their sparse larder with the abundant fish and game in the area.

Seth Bullock was one of those young men.[11] It was natural that he would want to visit the brand-new Yellowstone Park. After all, he was the delegate to the Montana territorial legislature who in December 1871 wrote a "memorial" asking the federal government to establish the park. The next summer, he became one of the first tourists to visit there.

Bullock had a colorful career. After serving in the Montana territorial legislature and as Lewis and Clark County sheriff, he moved to Deadwood, South Dakota, to set up a mercantile business. He became sheriff in Deadwood and befriended Theodore Roosevelt, a rancher who lived nearby. Later, when Roosevelt was elected president, he appointed Bullock as US marshal for the Dakota Territory.

Bullock left Helena for the park on horseback August 23, 1872, with three friends and a packhorse named "Judge Clancy," after the man who sold them the animal.

On the second night out, lightning spooked their horses, but they were able to catch a rope on Judge Clancy and stop the stampede. Lost horses were a common occurrence for Yellowstone travelers all through the period when horseback and wagon were the primary means of transportation. Since the travelers couldn't carry food for their horses, the animals needed to graze overnight, and sometimes they wandered off. Often, travel was delayed to search for horses, which were sometimes found miles away.

Bullock and his companions went to Mammoth Hot Springs, where they found what he described as "quite a colony of invalids" who "speak of the medicinal qualities of the hot springs with high praise."[12]

The men visited the Yellowstone Canyon, Falls, and Lake, then made their way to the geysers over Mary Mountain Trail. By the time they reached the Upper Geyser Basin, they were, as Bullock wrote, "running out of grub," with "nothing left but flour and coffee so they dined on a concoction of geyser water and flour they called 'Geyser Sauce.'"

When Bullock and his friends got back to Bottler's ranch in the Paradise Valley a week later, they dined on what he called "the first civilized grub that we had for twenty days."[13]

WOMEN BEGAN TOURING YELLOWSTONE PARK WHILE THE INK WAS STILL drying on the documents President Ulysses S. Grant signed to create it. One of them was Emma Stone of Bozeman, Montana.[14]

Emma, her husband, Hiram, and their two sons were visiting Mammoth Hot Springs, where they met two specimen hunters who offered to guide them through the park. Such men often hung around the hotel looking for clients to guide, but in just a few years enough tourists had passed to make trails clear, and such services were no longer needed.

The Stones left no written record of their trip, but what they did can be inferred. Because there were no roads, people had to travel on horseback along game trails and through forests so tall that they couldn't see the sky. Horses had to jump fallen timber that littered the ground. Sometimes trees were so close together that pack mules had to get on their knees to squeeze their wide loads under the lower branches. The Stones visited the Upper and

Lower Geyser Basins and Yellowstone Lake and Falls, making what historians call "a complete tour."

E. S. Topping, one of their guides, said, "It was a hard trip for the lady of the party, Mrs. Stone, but she now has the satisfaction of remembering that to her belongs the honor of being the first white woman to see the beauties of the National Park."[15]

Emma Stone's two sons apparently were in their teens when they toured Yellowstone Park with their parents, so credit for being the first white child to visit the park probably belongs to Mabel Cross Osmond.[16]

Mabel was just six years old when she went to the park with her parents in 1874. Mabel's father, Captain Robert Cross, was a Civil War veteran who came to Montana to be the post trader at Crow Agency, which was then located nine miles east of present-day Livingston, Montana.

Mabel wrote her memoir more than fifty years after her trip, but she still had vivid memories of it, including such details as the saddle she rode. "The blacksmith," she said, "taking a man's saddle, fastened a covered iron rod from the pommel around on the right side to the back. This rod and the seat were well padded with blankets. A covered stirrup, wide enough for my two feet was hung on the left side and across this open side from the pommel to the rod in back was attached a buckled leather strap so that, when mounted, I sat as a child in a high chair."[17]

Mabel rode an Indian pony she called "Dolly," which she said saved her life "by instantly stopping when, while descending a steep trail my saddle turned, leaving me hanging head downward, helplessly strapped in until the others could reach me."

The Crosses had an Army escort to see them through Indian country until they reached the Bottler ranch. Mabel recalled the stop clearly.

"We enjoyed one of Grandma Bottler's good dinners. I remember the cute little roast Pig with an ear of corn in its mouth, and also being awakened during the night by hearing her shrilly shouting—'Fredereek, Fredereek, the skunk is after the chickuns.' Though eighty years old, she kept her 'store teeth' put away—'fearing to wear them out'—she told us."[18]

Mabel got a ride on a new sailboat on Yellowstone Lake. She gorged herself with wild berries on an island and got sick on the boat trip to shore. She blamed the upset stomach on seasickness.

At Mammoth Hot Springs, Mabel's father made a basket out of her mother's corset stays and laid it in one of the pools. The running waters encrusted the item with white mineral deposits, making a souvenir that Mabel still had when she wrote her memoir.

Indians stole a band of horses the day before Sarah Tracy left Bozeman for Yellowstone Park in June of 1874.[19] But Mrs. Tracy was used to Indians. When she arrived in Bozeman in 1869 with her new husband, Bozeman pioneer W. H. Tracy, Indians were encamped on the south side of town. She said, "They would peer in the windows if the doors were locked, or come flocking around the door begging for biscuits, soap, clothes, everything."

Such encounters left Mrs. Tracy with little fear of Indians, but the commander at Fort Ellis still didn't want to let her party go to Yellowstone in the midst of "Indian troubles." Finally, after some haggling, he agreed to provide an armed escort.

Mrs. Tracy traveled to the park by stagecoach over the new toll road through Yankee Jim Canyon, which[20] was operated by Yankee Jim George, who took it over when its builders abandoned it. She said the view from the hill overlooking Mammoth Hot Springs was breathtaking, but the slope was so steep that the driver had to chain the wagon wheels. This "rough locking" caused the wagon to skid slowly down the hill, and it made for a rough ride.

She was greeted by several other women who were staying at McCartney's Hotel, which was just a crude log cabin. Mrs. Tracy waited for her husband at Mammoth for a week, then joined a party of fifteen to travel to the interior of the park.

Like Mabel Cross Osmond, Mrs. Tracy thought a highlight of her trip was a ride on the new sailboat that two men had recently finished on Yellowstone Lake. The men said they would let the first women to ride the boat have the honor of naming it. Mrs. Tracy and another woman named Sarah decided on the name "Sallie," after themselves. As a reward for their effort, the ladies were allowed to fry doughnuts in bear grease for the whole party.

Mrs. Tracy saw falls, canyons, lakes, and geysers. She said, "The balmy breezes and mountain sunshine had done our complexions to a turn. While our clothing was a little worse for wear, yet we had seen the Yellowstone National Park in its primitive beauty."[21]

During N. P. Langford's time as superintendent of Yellowstone National Park, most of the people who visited there came from adjacent territories.

But reports of Yellowstone's wonders had spread widely, and a few wealthy adventurers from distant places found the time and money to make the long trip. Big-game hunting, which was perfectly legal until the Army took over administration of the park in 1886, was a prime attraction.

One such traveler was Windham Thomas Wyndam-Quin, the fourth Earl of Dunraven. A wealthy Irish nobleman, Lord Dunraven hired several men to accompany him on a trip to the park in 1874.

One of them was Fredrick Bottler, a rancher who had settled in the Paradise Valley on the Yellowstone River in 1868. Bottler was familiar with Yellowstone's wonders and served as an outfitter, guide, and hunter for several early expeditions. Another was Texas Jack Omohundro, who hunted with Buffalo Bill Cody when he provided meat for railroad building and later was his partner in a popular stage play. Texas Jack continued on the stage after Buffalo Bill moved on.

Dunraven, who had been a war correspondent for British newspapers, was an astute observer with a droll wit. In addition to his stories about watching geysers and shooting trophy elk and dangerous grizzly bears, Dunraven told stories of packers trying to pack a cantankerous mule and of roasting fresh elk meat on a stick over a campfire. Dunraven's 1875 book, *The Great Divide*, helped popularize the park, especially in Europe.

High-ranking military officers also had the time and means to visit Yellowstone Park when it was still an untamed wilderness. One of them was General W. W. Belknap, President Ulysses S. Grant's secretary of war, who visited the park in the summer of 1875. Belknap invited four other generals to join him on his luxurious tour, including W. E. Strong, who provided a colorful account of the trip.[22]

The five generals crossed the country on the new transcontinental railroad in a plush Pullman car, smoking cigars, drinking whisky, and telling stories. Then they rode in a special stagecoach that traveled at breakneck speed from Utah to Montana.

Along the way, they were feted with banquets, parties, and parades. In Bozeman, a Silver Coronet Band greeted them at the edge of town and escorted them through the city to Fort Ellis.

At Fort Ellis, they were provided with an escort of active-duty soldiers led by Lieutenant Gustavus Doane, whose report of the Washburn Expedition was well known by military brass. Each general was assigned an orderly to take care of his every whim: packing his personal belongings, putting up his tent, rolling out his bed roll, digging his latrine, and cleaning any fish he caught. All at Army expense of course.

The generals spent their time viewing falls, lakes, and geysers, but more important to them were the thrills of the sportsman's paradise. They caught four-pound trout on light fishing tackle, hunted trophy elk, and even stampeded a buffalo herd.

While Langford's tenure as superintendent of Yellowstone Park was ending in 1877, tourists tangled with Indians there during what has been called "The Last Indian War." Several bands of Nez Perce had joined together and decided to leave their homeland on the Idaho-Washington-Oregon border to avoid being forced onto a reservation. They headed toward the buffalo country on the Montana plains, where they hoped to make a new life.

After several battles in Idaho, the Nez Perce made an agreement with Montana settlers that they would travel peacefully to the buffalo country. That agreement was shattered when the Army attacked a sleeping Nez Perce camp on the banks of the Big Hole River on August 9, 1877.

The Indians rallied and drove their attackers back into a hillside grove, where sharpshooters kept them pinned down. Meanwhile, the Nez Perce hastily buried their dead, packed, and fled. They went eastward into Idaho and circled back through Yellowstone Park, a route they apparently chose to avoid settled areas of Montana and especially the Army post at Fort Ellis east of Bozeman. Several tourist parties were visiting the park that summer and ran afoul of the Nez Perce. The stories of these tourists are detailed in the book *Encounters in Yellowstone* by M. Mark Miller.[23]

General William Tecumseh Sherman, whose famous March to the Sea is credited with winning the Civil War for the Union, visited the park in August 1877, just before the Nez Perce arrived there. He was commanding general of the entire US Army at the time, and his Yellowstone visit was a side trip while he was inspecting forts across the West.

Sherman knew the Nez Perce had entered Montana when he made his Yellowstone trip, but he trusted his subordinates to dispatch the matter quickly. He did keep his escort small to leave troops available to quell the Indians. He took four enlisted men from Fort Ellis along with a packer who also served as guide. They joined the men who had traveled with Sherman from Washington: his son and two colonels.

Sherman's party rushed through the park and paused only briefly to see such sights as Tower Fall and the Falls and Canyon of the Yellowstone. They spent only one day at what was Sherman's main objective, the grand geysers of the Upper Geyser Basin. They headed back just days before the Nez Perce arrived there. On their return trip, they heard about the bloody Big Hole Battle and rushed to Fort Ellis to learn details.

In the summer of 1877, Frank Carpenter and two of his friends ignored the news of Indian trouble in Idaho and left Helena on their way to Yellowstone Park. They had planned for just the three of them carrying their equipment and supplies on a packhorse and living off the land. But they stopped at Frank's parents' ranch near Radersburg, south of Helena. There, Frank's married sister, Emma Cowan, insisted on joining the party. By the time the Radersburg Party left for the park, it included Emma, her husband, her thirteen-year-old sister Ida, a carriage, a supply wagon with a hired driver and a cook, as well as Frank, his friends, and another Radersburg man.

The Radersburg Party was going to see the grand geysers that had intrigued Emma ever since she was a girl. She had visited Mammoth Hot Springs with her parents in 1874, but they didn't cross the park to geyserland.

The 1877 party traveled up the Missouri River, then up the Madison, and traversed Raynolds Pass to Henrys Lake, where they rested, hunted, and fished for several days. Then they proceeded over Targhee Pass to the park. This route that crossed the Continental Divide twice was easier than passing through the rugged middle canyon of the Madison.

The wagon road ended at the Lower Geyser Basin, so after a day of seeing the sights there, Emma and her companions cached their food and equipment and rode on horseback to the Upper Geyser Basin. While there, Emma's brother, Frank Carpenter, and his friends dumped hundreds of pounds of rubble down the mouth of Old Faithful just to see what would happen. They were greatly amused when the geyser erupted to about half its normal height and belched up tree stumps and rocks.

Carpenter wrote freely about stuffing Old Faithful in the book he published about his adventures, and Emma Cowan's husband, George, described adding his name alongside those he found on geological features and collecting specimens. These incidents show that even reputable citizens like members of the Radersburg Party felt free to abuse the park. George Cowan was then the county attorney of Jefferson County, Montana.

Frank and two of his friends decided to see Yellowstone Lake, Falls, and Canyon, and they rode away, leaving the rest of the Radersburg Party at the Upper Geyser Basin, where they enjoyed geyserland for five days. Frank and his companions agreed to meet them at the Lower Geyser basin.

After Frank and his companions rejoined the party, they decided to head home and celebrated the decision by cavorting around a big bonfire—a fire that a Nez Perce named Yellow Wolf saw and pointed out to his companions.

The morning after the bonfire, Nez Perce entered the Radersburg Party camp. The party hastily packed up and headed down the Firehole River, accompanied by a large Indian contingent. Another group of Nez Perce forced the party to turn around and head up Nez Perce Creek to confer with the chief who was in charge at the time.

The chief forced them to trade their fine horses for worn-out Indian ponies and sent them on their way. The chief was trying to protect the tourists, but they were subsequently attacked by a group of Nez Perce he didn't control.

George Cowan was shot twice, once in the head, and left for dead. Emma Cowan, her sister, and her brother, Frank Carpenter, were taken captive, and the rest of the party fled into the surrounding timber. Although terrified, Emma and her siblings were treated well. On the third day of their captivity, a council of chiefs met and decided to release the trio into the Yellowstone wilderness.

Emma and her siblings struggled down the Yellowstone River, past the canyon and falls, and over Dunraven Pass. They finally found a group of Army scouts, who took them to Mammoth Hot Springs. Emma and Ida returned home while Frank went back to the park to look for Emma's husband. The Army rescued the rest of the Radersburg Party as they headed back to civilization.

When George came to and tried to stand, a lone Indian shot him again and left. He was unable to walk, so he crawled six miles looking for help. Eventually, Army scouts found him lying exhausted by the road. The Army hauled George across the park on rough roads freshly hacked from the wilderness. After George's bone-jarring ride, he was taken to Bottler's ranch, and Emma raced there overnight from Helena to be with him.

About the time the Radersburg Party reached the Upper Geyser Basin, three groups of young men left Helena for the park.[24] The groups combined at

Mammoth Hot Springs, making up what was called the Helena Party. They proceeded to visit the Grand Canyon of the Yellowstone and the Upper and Lower Falls. South of the falls, they saw the main band of six hundred Nez Perce crossing the Yellowstone River, beat a hasty retreat, and went into hiding.

The next morning, Andrew Weikert, the most experienced outdoorsman of the group and its de facto leader, went with another man, Leslie Wilkie, to see if the Indians had moved on. They found the place where the Nez Perce had crossed the Yellowstone River and determined that the Indians were gone, deeming it safe for the Helena Party to resume the trip.

While the two men were returning to camp, Weikert saw an Indian peeking over a log. He warned Wilkie, turned his horse, and raced for the timber as the Nez Perce set loose a barrage of rifle fire. Weikert escaped injury in the first round of fire, but he was creased in the shoulder in the second round, and another rifle ball splintered his gun stock. His horse stumbled, and Weikert somersaulted over its head.

Weikert landed with his rifle in his hand. He said he raised his gun and "up and let them have one from my repeater, and you ought to have seen them dodge."[25] Weikert remounted his horse and rode to where Wilkie waited. The pair rode into the timber as far as they could, then dismounted and walked. Wilkie bandaged Weikert's shoulder, and they made their way through the timber. When Weikert and Wilkie were confident the Indians had gone, they retrieved their horses and rode on.

They called out as they approached the camp where their friends should have been waiting. There was no answer, and Weikert and Wilkie rode into a desolate scene. Nez Perce scouts had attacked the camp and driven the Helena Party into the forest. The Indians took whatever arms and equipment they wanted and burned the rest. They also stole fourteen horses, which was probably the main goal of the raid.

As Weikert and Wilkie rode back toward Mammoth Hot Springs, they caught up with several of their companions and helped them to safety. Other members of the Helena Party finally made their way back to Mammoth, but when three men didn't return, Weikert decided to look for them.

The owner of the cabin at Mammoth, James McCartney, agreed to go with him. Most of the refugees had left McCartney's for Bozeman, but three stayed behind, including Richard Dietrich, a Helena music teacher who had promised one of the missing men's mother that he would look after her son.

As Weikert was leaving, he jokingly promised Dietrich a proper burial if the Nez Perce attacked him. It was a promise Weikert would have to keep.

Weikert and McCartney returned to the campsite where the Nez Perce had attacked their friends and buried the body of Charles Kenck. They searched for the two other missing men but concluded that they must have escaped and run southward.

On their way back to Mammoth Hot Springs, Weikert and McCartney saw a group of eighteen Nez Perce approaching them two hundred yards away. Seeing they were outnumbered, the men raced toward the nearest brush. The Indians fired rifles at them.

Weikert said, "We'd hear the balls whistle through the air and see them pick up the dust."[26] The men returned fire, and Weikert said they "made some good Indians," a reference to General Philip Sheridan's dictum that the only good Indian is a dead Indian.

The Nez Perce got off their horses and continued to fire from behind a pile of rocks. A bullet hit Weikert's horse. When he dismounted, he saw blood gushing from the animal's side, bade it goodbye, and ran.

The Indians kept shooting—at least fifty times—but Weikert said the only shot that came close tore a piece out of his boot leg. The two men paused while McCartney took off his spurs so he could run. He threw them under a fallen log in hopes of retrieving them later.

Weikert and McCartney made it into the brush. The Indians didn't follow because a hidden man could easily pick off an attacker. Weikert said, "They were terrible brave so long as they had the advantage, but just as soon as the tables were turned, they made themselves scarce behind the hills."[27]

When Weikert and McCartney were sure the Indians had gone, they started walking toward Mammoth Hot Springs. When they approached the cabin there, it was dark and the door was open. They went in and lit a candle and saw the body of Richard Dietrich. Yellow Wolf, the young Indian who captured John Shively, said later that one of his companions had shot Dietrich while he stood in the cabin doorway. Weikert and McCartney couldn't find the other men who had stayed behind and concluded they must have escaped.

Weikert and McCartney couldn't find any food in the cabin, so they decided to walk toward Bozeman. They finally came to an Army camp, where they were fed and a surgeon tended to Weikert's wound.

The next day, Weikert returned to McCartney's cabin with a contingent of soldiers and citizens to bury Dietrich in a temporary grave. Weikert said, "We buried him the best we could in an old bath tub that was at the Springs, for lumber was scarce."[28] Weikert then returned to his home near Helena to rest and recover from his wounded shoulder.

Six week later, Weikert returned to the park to retrieve the bodies of Charles Kenck and Richard Dietrich. He had to haul Kenck's body on a packhorse for fifty miles and Dietrich's about half that to get them to a point that could be reached by a wagon.

"It was about as lonely a ride as I ever took,"[29] he said of his return trip to Helena. There, a music society that Dietrich had founded took care of his funeral arrangements and burial.

Weikert said, "Dietrich was a particular friend of mine, and I kept good the promise I made him the last time I saw him in giving him a decent burial."[30]

The Army tried to contain the Nez Perce in Yellowstone Park, but the Indians outmaneuvered them and made their way to the Montana plains. When the Nez Perce learned they could not stay in Montana, they headed to Canada to join Sitting Bull and his coalition of Sioux and Cheyenne. The Army caught up with the Indians just forty miles from the Canadian border and defeated them at the Battle of the Bear Paw. That's where Chief Joseph gave his famous "I will fight no more forever" speech on October 5, 1877.

People seeking concessions in the park continued to press their applications with the US Congress and the secretary of the interior. Also, there were complaints about souvenir collectors destroying geological features and hunters decimating wildlife. Such complaints came from a wide range of people, including Montana territorial governor Benjamin Potts, a group of citizens from Bozeman, and Harry Horr, who owned a hotel with James McCartney at Mammoth Hot Springs. Gilman Sawtell, who homesteaded at Henrys Lake west of the park and provided accommodations there for tourists, complained that Langford rarely visited the park and said he would make a better superintendent because he lived nearby.

By 1877, dissatisfaction with N. P. Langford's tenure as Yellowstone National Park superintendent began to boil over. Commercial hunters were slaughtering big game in the park to feed the nation's voracious appetite for leather to run belt-driven mills and factories. Specimen collectors were smashing geological features to collect objects for sale. Tourists were carving their names on geyser cones and trees and harvesting flowers. Under Langford, no concessions had been granted, nor had roads or hotels been built.

Among the people who sought to replace Langford as park superintendent were the Henrys Lake homesteader Gilman Sawtell and Lieutenant Gustavus Doane. Philetus Norris, who had tried to document Yellowstone's wonders just months before the Washburn Expedition, got the job.

Norris immediately took up residence near the park, promulgated regulations forbidding specimen collection and defacement of geological features, and began building a road from Mammoth Hot Springs to the Lower Geyser Basin. The Northern Pacific finished its transcontinental railroad in 1882 and started building a spur line to the park. The year after the railroad arrived, the number of visits jumped from one thousand to five thousand.

Despite Norris's best efforts, roads in the park remained crude and despoliation of wildlife and geological features continued. Things got so bad that the secretary of the interior asked the Army to take over administration of Yellowstone Park.

When troops arrived in 1886, they ended hunting in the park and even forbade carrying guns there. The US Army Corps of Engineers arrived with the intent of making roads in the park the best in the United States. Soon, Yellowstone Park was transformed from a wilderness preserve for the wealthy and the well connected from afar to a pleasuring ground for the middle class.

CHAPTER ELEVEN

Fame and Obscurity

While N. P. Langford was securing his reputation as the discoverer of Yellowstone National Park, Lieutenant Gustavus Doane continued his Army career and tried to enhance his fame by undertaking more explorations. Doane completed writing the first official government description of the wonders of the Yellowstone on December 15, 1870, and it was presented to Congress on February 24, 1871. It won him high praise. The Army engineer and Yellowstone historian Hiram Chittenden said, "His fine descriptions have never been surpassed by any subsequent writer. Although suffering intense physical pain during the greater portion of the trip, it did not extinguish in him the truly poetic with which those strange phenomena seem to have inspired in him."[1]

Doane's report doubtless contributed to the demands for him to serve various expeditions and dignitaries as a Yellowstone Park guide. He accompanied the first official government expeditions to explore the area in 1871. That was a combined effort, with Ferdinand Vandiveer Hayden leading a group of civilians and Captains John W. Barlow and David P. Heap leading an Army contingent. The expeditions provided detailed descriptions of the area and maps that were used to persuade the US Congress to establish Yellowstone Park, the world's first national park. Doane also guided a tour by US Secretary of War W. W. Belknap in 1875.

Inspired by reports of Henry Stanley's search for David Livingstone in Africa, Doane proposed an exploration of the Nile to the Smithsonian in 1874, but the secretary of war turned it down.

Doane still thought he could earn fame as an explorer, and in 1876 he obtained permission to launch a risky winter exploration of the Snake River. He took his soldiers across the Yellowstone Plateau in early winter with pack mules carrying the parts of a boat that was designed to be assembled on-site. Cold and accumulated snow made travel difficult, and the expedition didn't reach Yellowstone Lake until October 24. Rough weather on the lake proved too much for the boat, so it didn't speed up travel as Doane hoped it would. The party hauled the boat to Heart Lake, which is drained by the Heart River, a tributary of the Snake. When Doane finally got the boat to the Snake, he found it wasn't tough enough for the big river's whitewater and had to be abandoned. Doane's superiors recalled the expedition, and he arrived back at Fort Ellis on February 2, 1877.

In 1880, the Army agreed to an expedition to explore the North Pole near Greenland, and Doane was granted permission to join it. However, the Army withdrew support after it was discovered that plans called for an unseaworthy ship. Private funding was secured for the expedition, and the ship headed north in July 1881. A heavy gale damaged the ship in August, and the expedition was scrapped. Doane's report stated that it accomplished nothing.

Between his explorations, Doane was active in the last of the Indian wars. In 1876, he was part of the Montana Column that was sent to meet Colonel George Armstrong Custer and help subdue Sitting Bull's coalition of Sioux and Cheyenne. On June 25, Custer decided to attack the Indians' encampment, with disastrous results. The Montana Column arrived on June 27 after the Indians had wiped out Custer and his men. Doane rigged stretchers carried by horses, and his troops used them to move survivors from Major Marcus Reno's forces to safety and medical care at a steamboat waiting on the Yellowstone River.

A year later, in the summer of 1877, the year the Nez Perce fled their homeland to avoid being forced onto a reservation, Doane was in charge of recruiting and training Crow Indian scouts for the Army. He hoped to engage the Nez Perce with his cavalry company assisted by sixty Crow, but conflicting orders from different superior officers prevented that. Doane did lead his men up the Yellowstone River and was sometimes credited with blocking the Nez Perce from escaping that way. But apparently the Nez Perce had always intended to exit the northeast corner of the park.

Doane was promoted to captain in September 1884 and moved to the Presidio in San Francisco, but his stay there was short. In February 1885, the Army assigned his company to Fort Bowie in Arizona to help capture Geronimo, who had gone off his reservation. Doane did not participate directly in the pursuit of Geronimo, who surrendered on September 4. By mid-October, Doane and his men were back at the Presidio.

By the mid-1880s Yellowstone Park was in the midst of what some writers called a "holocaust." Sportsmen looking for trophies and hide hunters striving to accommodate the leather market were decimating big-game animals, and specimen collectors were destroying geological features. In September 1886, the secretary of the interior asked the Army to take over administration of the park and end the mayhem.

Doane wrote letters to his commanders and to US congressmen lobbying for the job of park superintendent. He claimed he was entitled to the job "by right of discovery" and even got the Montana legislature to support his application. But the secretary of war chose another officer for the job.

Embittered and with his health failing, Doane sought retirement in February 1892 and went back to Bozeman, Montana, on six months' medical leave. He caught influenza in April and died there on May 5, 1892. Montana newspapers covered his death, but it received little notice elsewhere. His obituary in the *Helena Daily Herald* said, "His were the first published letters concerning the Yellowstone National Park," but the story didn't mention the Washburn Expedition or his formal report. Perhaps if it had, his death might have received wider notice. The *Herald* obituary does list Doane's participation in the expedition to the North Pole and his attempt to explore the Snake River.

His widow, Mary Hunter Doane, lived another sixty years and worked to enhance her husband's reputation. She donated an extensive collection of his papers to the Montana State University Library.

Members of the Washburn Expedition named a mountain (now called Colter Peak) in Doane's honor, and Ferdinand Hayden named another peak after him. In 2018, Native Americans asked that Mount Doane be renamed First Peoples Mountain because of Doane's role in the Marias Massacre.

WHEN MEMBERS OF THE WASHBURN EXPEDITION CAME HOME, THEY returned to their previous endeavors. They were chosen for the trip because of their prominence, so it's no surprise that several of them moved on to distinguished careers. Others, of course, died in relative obscurity.

General Henry Dana Washburn knew he was in fragile health when he agreed to join the 1870 expedition that bears his name. A snowstorm dumped nearly two feet of snow on the party while they searched for Truman Everts on the southeast side of Yellowstone Lake, and General Washburn caught a cold that aggravated his consumption.

He returned home to Helena. Despite his weakness, he was able to write an account of the trip that the *New York Times* praised for its "most graphic and effective descriptions of actual scenery," noting that "no unstudied descriptions that we have read of the internal scenery of the American Continent surpass his notes in any particular."[2] A few months later, ill health forced him to return home to Indiana in January 1871. He was put to bed at the home of his father-in-law and died a few days later.

After the return of the Washburn Expedition, Truman Everts searched for a job in Montana for a few weeks, but by midsummer he decided to return to the East. He took his grown daughter Elizabeth, or "Bessie," with him, so Helena lost one of its few eligible belles. Nobody knows if Warren Gillette tried to court her that summer.

Everts never paid the reward that had been offered for his rescue. Years later, his rescuer, Yellowstone Jack Baronett, visited Everts in New York, but the meeting apparently didn't go well. Baronett later said he wished he "had let the son-of-a-gun roam."[3]

Everts's account of his ordeal when he was lost in the Yellowstone wilderness was published the next year in the November 1871 issue of *Scribner's Monthly*. The article brought him substantial acclaim, and there was sentiment for making him the first superintendent of Yellowstone Park, but he wouldn't take the job without a salary.

About 1880, Everts married a fourteen-year-old girl and the couple settled on a farm in Maryland. Their son, Truman Everts Jr., was born in 1891, when Everts was seventy-five.

Little was known about Everts's later life until his son came to the Yellowstone Park Research Center in 1961, where he was interviewed. The elder Everts worked for the Post Office Department and died in 1901.

The charter for Warren Gillette's profitable toll road ran out in 1875, and he turned to managing his two-thousand-acre sheep ranch, where he raised merinos and helped popularize the breed. A Republican, Gillette served two terms in the lower chamber of the territorial legislature and one in the upper chamber and was a member of the convention that wrote Montana's first state constitution. He never married and died at the home of his nephew in Helena in 1912.

Sam Hauser resumed management of his business empire, which included mines, smelters, banks, and ranches. He also oversaw the building of the Utah and Northern Railway in Montana.

Hauser was a Democrat and attended the 1884 National Convention that nominated Grover Cleveland for president. Cleveland appointed Hauser as governor of Montana Territory in 1905. Hauser continued to devote most of his time to his business and resigned the governorship after about a year and a half. He died in Helena at the home of his son in November 1914.

After the return of the Washburn Expedition, Cornelius Hedges remained a lifelong advocate for Yellowstone Park, writing in favor of its establishment and speaking at ceremonies commemorating its founding. He was also active in governmental and civic affairs. In 1871, President Ulysses S. Grant appointed him US attorney for Montana. He served two terms as Montana superintendent of schools and was a probate court judge for more than ten years. In 1884, Hedges was a member of the Constitutional Convention for Montana statehood.

He was active in the Montana Historical Society and served as its recording secretary from 1875 to 1885. He spent the last years of his life almost entirely in service of the Masonic Order, holding high and influential offices in that organization.

When Hedges died in 1897, the *Helena Daily Record* wrote, "No better man has ever lived in Montana, nor to any is there a higher mead of praise for what he did and gave to Montana."[4]

Jake Smith didn't tarry long in Montana after he came back to Helena from the Washburn Expedition. In 1872, his wife insisted that he return to San Francisco. He became a broker there, and by 1882 he was a millionaire. But he lost his fortune, and in 1885 his wife left him and took their four children back east. She divorced him in 1892.

Clearly, Smith was not the wastrel that N. P. Langford portrayed him to be. Instead, he was a shrewd businessman who sometimes hit hard luck. The noted Yellowstone Park historian Aubrey Haines observed that "it is quite probable Jake's 'good-natured nonsense' and keenly perceptive wit barbed the dignified Langford." It also seems possible that Langford portrayed Smith as a scamp simply to spice up his 1905 book about the Washburn Expedition. Smith died in 1897 in San Francisco.[5]

Benjamin Stickney bought a mining claim after he returned from the Washburn Expedition, then resumed freighting. He sold his freighting business and began ranching in Craig, about forty-five miles north of Helena. Stickney married and had three children. He eventually owned a large ranch, had an interest in a ferry across the Missouri River, and ran a store in Craig. He died in Florida in 1912.

After the Washburn Expedition, Walter Trumbull wrote articles describing what he had seen for the Helena *Rocky Mountain Gazette* and the *Overland Monthly*. He became a correspondent for the *Helena Herald* and accompanied William H. Clagett during his campaign to be Montana Territory delegate to the US Congress. Doubtless this provided Trumbull with opportunities to help persuade Clagett to introduce the legislation in 1871 that eventually led to the establishment of Yellowstone National Park. Trumbull probably also garnered the support of his father, the influential US senator Lyman Trumbull.

In 1879, Walter Trumbull was appointed assistant consul to Zanzibar, a collection of islands off the east coast of Africa that was a thriving trade center. There, he caught consumption, which forced him to return to the United States. His physician told him to move to New Mexico to improve his health. He was admitted to the Arizona bar, but his health continued to deteriorate and he returned east for treatment in sanitariums in New York and Michigan. He died in 1891 at his father's home in Springfield, Illinois.

Jack Baronett was not a member of the Washburn Expedition, but he became prominent in their story by rescuing Truman Everts. A year after the expedition, he made another important mark on Yellowstone Park history by building the first bridge across the Yellowstone River about two hundred yards above where the Lamar River runs into the Yellowstone. It was a toll bridge built for miners and freighters traveling back and forth to the mines at Cooke City, on the northeast edge of the park. The Nez Perce tried to burn the bridge when they fled through the park in 1877, but it was rebuilt. Baronett let his partners operate the bridge while he guided hunting parties, scouted for the Army, and prospected for gold throughout the West.

Although Baronett had been in the Confederate army, he did work for Army officers including General Philip Sheridan, who hired him several times, and President Ulysses S. Grant's secretary of war, General W. W. Belknap.[6] General W. E. Strong, who chronicled Belknap's tour in 1875, said

Baronett was "famous as an Indian fighter and hunter, he is still more celebrated as a guide."[7]

Baronett was considered for the job of park superintendent in 1884, and, when the Army took over administration of Yellowstone Park in 1886, he was hired as assistant superintendent. But the Army took his bridge from him without compensation in 1894. He had invested $15,000 in the bridge and sued for compensation. After legal battles that cost him $6,000, he was granted compensation of $5,000.

Baronett invested the $5,000 in an expedition to the Alaska gold rush, but his ship was crushed in arctic ice. He survived the shipwreck and returned to Seattle. He continued prospecting in the West and died in 1906.

The members of the Washburn Expedition were chosen for their prominence and credibility. Their life stories after the expedition show that they were chosen well.

Two ambitious men, N. P. Langford and Gustavus Cheney Doane, sought to win fame and fortune by documenting the wonders at the headwaters of the Yellowstone and Madison Rivers. Based on the reports of dozens of people who had traveled to the area, they were confident they would find towering waterfalls, a huge mountain lake, hot springs, and geysers. Langford and Doane weren't disappointed, but their contribution wasn't discovery or even documentation. It was publicity.

The publicity was enough to persuade the US Congress to fund a large civilian expedition to explore the area and for the Army to send surveyors. Their reports were finished by 1872, when serious efforts were launched to persuade the US Congress to set the area aside as a national park. The effort was successful, and on March 1, 1872, President Ulysses S. Grant signed the law creating the world's first national park.

The park developed little during Langford's five-year tenure as the park's first superintendent. He was replaced in 1877 and returned to Saint Paul, Minnesota, where he became a prominent banker and head of the Minnesota Historical Society. When he died, newspapers across the country lauded him as the "Discoverer of Yellowstone Park."

Doane continued his Army career, serving in some of the last Indian wars. He tried twice to be named superintendent of Yellowstone Park but was rebuffed both times. He died in relative obscurity on May 5, 1892.

Both N. P. Langford and Gustavus Doane played significant roles in bringing the wonders at the headwaters of the Yellowstone and Madison Rivers to public attention. They helped in the creation of the world's first national park as a place to preserve wilderness and provide enjoyment, an idea that caught on. Today, there are hundreds of national parks in the United States and around the world.

NOTES

PREFACE

1. Langford 1905.
2. Langford 1905, 128.
3. Gillette.

CHAPTER ONE: MOUNTAIN MEN GET NO RESPECT

1. Haines 1996, 101.
2. A complete version of Cook and Folsom's manuscript was unavailable for 143 years, and it was thought all copies had been lost in fires. A complete copy was found in 2013 and is in the Merrill G. Burlingame Collections at the Montana State University Library.
3. Haines 1974, 4.
4. Potts.
5. Loc. cit.
6. Victor, 75.
7. Haines 1974, 10–11.
8. Russell, 100.
9. For example, Aubrey Haines, *The Journal of a Trapper* (University of Nebraska Press, 1965).
10. Dunraven, 211.
11. Current estimates put the length of Yellowstone Lake at 19.9 miles.
12. Gunnison, 151.
13. Raynolds, 10.
14. Doubtless the man was Gilman Sawtell, who had settled at Henrys Lake, Idaho, in the 1860s.
15. Cowan, 157–58.
16. Schullery, 16.
17. Dunraven, 136.
18. DeLacy.
19. Cook, Folsom, and Peterson, 54.
20. Haines 1974, 48.

21. Loc. cit.
22. Haines 1974, 64.
23. Loc. cit.

CHAPTER TWO: RECRUITING GOOD MEN

1. Haines 1974, 62.
2. Langford 1972, viii.
3. Stuart.
4. Langford 1972, xxxvi.
5. Langford 1972, xx.
6. Langford 1972, xxxix.
7. The *Helena Herald* published both daily and weekly editions. References to the newspaper in general are listed as *Helena Herald*; references to the daily edition are *Helena Daily Herald* and to the weekly edition, *Helena Weekly Herald*.
8. Gillette.
9. Langford 1974, xli.
10. Langford 1974, xxxix.

CHAPTER THREE: INTO THE WILDERNESS

1. Langford 1872, 4.
2. Gillette, 15.
3. Loc. cit.
4. Gillette, 17.
5. Gillette, 18.
6. Langford 1972, 1.
7. Doane, 2.
8. Langford 1972, 14.
9. Langford 1972, 5.
10. Langford 1972, c9.9.
11. Loc. cit.
12. Langford 1905, 10.
13. Doane, 3.
14. Gillette, 17.
15. Doane, 3.
16. Langford 1905, 8.
17. Loc. cit.

18. Loc. cit.
19. Gillette, 26.
20. Doane, 6.
21. Loc. cit.
22. Langford 1871, 7–8.
23. Langford 1905, 80.
24. Loc. cit.
25. Langford 1905, 81.
26. Loc. cit.
27. Langford 1905, 80.
28. Doane, 8.
29. Langford 1871, 8.
30. Trumbull, 482.
31. Loc. cit.

CHAPTER FOUR: FALLS AND CANYONS

1. Langford 1905, 19
2. The official height of Tower Fall now is 132 feet.
3. Doane, 8.
4. Langford 1905, 85.
5. Doane, 8.
6. Doane, 9.
7. Loc. cit.
8. Gillette, 18.
9. Doane, 10.
10. Langford gave the elevation at 9,800 feet. The official elevation today is 10,223 feet.
11. Langford 1871, 10.
12. Loc. cit.
13. Loc. cit.
14. Langford 1871, 11.
15. Loc. cit.
16. Washburn, *Helena Daily Herald*, September 27 and 28, 1870.
17. Langford 1905, 95.
18. Loc. cit.
19. Langford 1905, 91.

20. Doane, 12.
21. Washburn, *Helena Daily Herald*, September 27 and 28, 1870.
22. Langford 1905, 172.
23. Doane, 12.
24. Washburn, 435.
25. Trumbull, 482.
26. Langford 1871, 12.
27. Doane, 14.
28. Loc. cit.
29. Loc. cit.
30. Washburn, *Helena Daily Herald*, September 27 and 28, 1870.
31. Langford 1905, 202.

CHAPTER FIVE: EVERTS GETS LOST

1. Langford 1871, 13.
2. Hedges, 381.
3. Langford 1871, 15.
4. Langford 1871, 16.
5. Doane, 17.
6. Doane, 18,
7. Langford 1905, 110.
8. Langford 1871, 113.
9. Langford 1905, 115.
10. Loc. cit.
11. Loc. cit.
12. Doane, 21.
13. Langford 1905, 124.
14. Langford 1871, 117.
15. The name was later changed to Colter Peak and another mountain was named for Langford.
16. Langford 1905, 136.
17. Langford 1905, 134.
18. Trumbull, 491.
19. Langford 1905, 135.
20. Doane, 22.
21. Langford 1905, 133.

CHAPTER SIX: EVERTS'S ORDEAL

1. Everts, 2.
2. Loc. cit.
3. Loc. cit.
4. Everts, 3.
5. Loc. cit.
6. Loc. cit.
7. Loc. cit.
8. Loc. cit.
9. Loc. cit.
10. Loc. cit.
11. Everts, 4.
12. Loc. cit.
13. Everts, 5.
14. Everts, 6.
15. Loc. cit.
16. Loc. cit.
17. Everts, 7.
18. Loc. cit.
19. Everts, 8.
20. Loc. cit.
21. Everts, 9
22. Everts, 10.
23. Loc. cit.
24. Everts, 11.
25. Loc. cit.
26. Loc. cit.
27. Loc. cit.
28. Everts, 12.
29. Loc. cit.
30. Everts, 13.
31. Loc. cit.
32. Everts, 15.
33. Everts, 16.
34. Loc. cit.

CHAPTER SEVEN: SEARCHING FOR EVERTS

1. Doane, 23.
2. Loc. cit.
3. Hedges, *Helena Daily Herald*, November 9, 1871.
4. Langford 1905, 145.
5. Hedges, *Helena Daily Herald*, November 9, 1871.
6. Loc. cit.
7. *Helena Daily Herald*, November 9, 1870.
8. Langford 1871, 119.
9. Langford 1905, 146.
10. Langford 1905, 147.
11. Langford 1871, 120.
12. Doane, 25.
13. Loc. cit.
14. Doane, 25–26. In this era it was common practice to let forest fires burn until they were extinguished by snow.
15. Doane, 26.
16. Langford 1905, 157.
17. Loc. cit.
18. Doane, 26.
19. Loc. cit.
20. Langford 1905, 165.
21. Langford 1905, 158.
22. Langford 1905, 155.
23. Langford 1904, 159.
24. Langford 1905, 162.
25. Langford 1905, 163.
26. Langford 1905, 100.
27. Gillette, 26.
28. Gillette, 28.
29. Loc. cit.
30. Gillette, 29.
31. Quoted in Haines 1996, 132.
32. Loc. cit.
33. Everts, 16.
34. Loc. cit.

CHAPTER EIGHT: GEYSERLAND AND HOME

1. Langford 1905, 100.
2. Langford 1905, 168.
3. Langford 1905, 169.
4. Langford 1905, 183.
5. Langford 1905, 184.
6. Schullery and Whittlesey, 24.
7. Doane, 34.
8. Doane, 35.

CHAPTER NINE: PERSUADING THE WORLD

1. Langford 1871, 128.
2. Trumbull, 495.
3. Haines 1974, 93.
4. Loc. cit.
5. Secretary of Interior Columbus Delano to Hayden, May 1, 1871.
6. Haines 1974, 129.
7. Reprinted in the *Chicago Tribune*, September 1, 1871.
8. The memorial is reprinted in full in the *Helena Weekly Herald*, February 8, 1871.
9. Moran's famous eight-by-fifteen-foot oil painting of the Grand Canyon of the Yellowstone was not completed until later.
10. Langford 1905, xxii.
11. Wheeler, 664.
12. Loc. cit.
13. Report 26 (to accompany House Bill H.R. 764, House of Representatives, 42d Congress, 2d session).
14. Quoted in Haines 1974, 121.
15. Langford 1905, 151.
16. Report 26 (to accompany House Bill H.R. 764, House of Representatives, 42d Congress, 2d session).

CHAPTER TEN: SUPERINTENDENT LANGFORD

1. Haines 1995, 214.
2. Langford 1905, xxiv.

3. Langford 1905, 49.

4. Haines, 1996, 14.

5. Black, 383.

6. The first Yellowstone Park travel guide was published by Harry J. Norton in Virginia City in 1873.

7. Raymond, 189.

8. Raymond, 289.

9. Clawson, passim.

10. Loc. cit.

11. Bullock, unnumbered.

12. Loc. cit.

13. Loc. cit.

14. Stone's story is described in Topping.

15. Topping, 95.

16. Osmond, undated.

17. Loc. cit.

18. Loc. cit.

19. Sarah Tracy's reminiscence is in the archives of the Museum of the Rockies in Bozeman.

20. Tracy, n.p.

21. Loc. cit.

22. Strong, 5.

23. Miller.

24. The combined group was called "The Helena Party." Their adventures are told in Weikert.

25. Weikert, 161.

26. Weikert, 70

27. Weikert, 171.

28. Weikert, 174.

29. Loc. cit.

30. Loc. cit.

CHAPTER ELEVEN: FAME AND OBSCURITY

1. Chittenden, 84.

2. Quoted in the *Helena Daily Herald*, October 27, 1870.

3. Quoted in Haines 1974, 139.

4. Quoted in Haines 1974, 145.
5. Haines 1974, 148.
6. Belknap was later impeached for a kickback scheme, but he was acquitted.
7. Strong, 43.

REFERENCES

Black, George. *Empire of Shadows.* New York: St. Martin's Press, 2012.

Bullock, Seth. *A Memorable Trip to Yellowstone National Park from Helena.* Montana Historical Society Archives, 1872.

Chittenden, Hiram Martin. *The Yellowstone National Park: Historical and Descriptive.* Cincinnati: Robert Clarke Company, 1903.

Clawson, Calvin C. *A Ride to the Infernal Regions: Yellowstone's First Tourists.* Eugene Lee Silliman, ed. Helena, MT: Riverbend Publishing, 2003.

Cook, Charles W., David E. Folsom, and William Peterson. *The Valley of the Upper Yellowstone.* Aubrey L. Haines, ed. Norman: University of Oklahoma Press, 1965.

Cowan, Mrs. George F. [Emma]. "Reminiscences of a Pioneer Life." *Contributions to the Historical Society of Montana,* vol. 4 (1903), 156–87.

DeLacy, Walter W. "A Trip Up the South Snake River in 1863." *Contributions to the Historical Society of Montana,* vol. 1 (1902), 100–127.

Doane, Gustavus C. *Report of Lieutenant Gustavus C. Doane upon the So-Called Yellowstone Expedition of 1870* (41st Cong., 34d Sess; Senate Exec. Doc. 51). Washington, DC: Govt. Printing Office, 1871.

Dunraven, The Earl of. *The Great Divide: Travels in the Upper Yellowstone in the Summer of 1874.* Lincoln,UK: Chatto and Windus, Piccadilly, 1876.

Everts, Truman. "Thirty-Seven Days of Peril." *Scribner's Monthly,* vol. 3 (November 1871), 1–17.

Folsom, David E. "The Folsom-Cook Explorations of the Upper Yellowstone in the Year 1869." *Contributions to the Historical Society of Montana,* vol. 5 (1904), 349–69.

Gillette, Warren. "The Quest of Warren Gillette: Based on the Original Diary." Brian Cockhill, ed. *Montana, the Magazine of Western History,* vol. 22, no. 3 (1972), 12–30.

Gunnison, J. W. *A History of the Mormons.* Philadelphia: Lippincott, Grambo & Co., 1852.

Haines, Aubrey L. *Yellowstone National Park: Its Exploration and Establishment.* Washington, DC: US Department of Interior, 1974.

Haines, Aubrey L. *The Yellowstone Story: History of Our First National Park.* Boulder: University Press of Colorado, 1996 (revised).

Hedges, Cornelius. "Journal of Judge Cornelius Hedges." *Contributions to the Historical Society of Montana,* vol. 4 (1904), 370–94.

Langford, Nathaniel P. *Vigilante Days and Ways.* Boston: J. C. Cupples Co., 1890.

Langford, Nathaniel P. "Wonders of the Yellowstone." *Scribner's Monthly,* vol. 2 (May), 1–15 (June), 113–28, 1871.

Langford, Nathaniel P. *The Discovery of Yellowstone Park 1870.* Saint Paul: J. E. Haynes, 1905.

Langford, Nathaniel Pitt Langford. *The Discovery of Yellowstone Park.* Lincoln: University of Nebraska, 1972.

Miller, M. Mark. *Encounters in Yellowstone.* Helena, MT: TwoDot, 2019.

Osmond, Mabel Cross. Typescript copy of her reminiscence at the Gallatin History Museum, Bozeman, Montana.

Potts, Daniel T. to Robert Potts. July 8, 1827, manuscript. Yellowstone Research Center.

Raymond, Rossiter. *Camp and Cabin.* New York: Fords, Howard & Hulber, 1880.

Raynolds, W. F. *Exploration of the Yellowstone.* US Government Printing Office, 1868.

Russell, Osborne. *Journal of a Trapper, or, Nine Years in the Rocky Mountains, 1834–1843.* Boise, ID: Syms-York, 1921.

Schullery, Paul. "Yellowstone's Ecological Holocaust." *Montana, the Magazine of Western History,* vol. 4 (Autumn 1997), 16–22.

Schullery, Paul, and Lee Whittlesey. *Myth and History in the Creation of Yellowstone National Park.* Lincoln: University of Nebraska Press, 2011.

Strong, W. E. *A Trip to the Yellowstone National Park in July, August, and September.* Washington, DC: Self-published, 1876.

Stuart, Granville. "A Memoir of the Life of James Stuart." *Contributions to the Historical Society of Montana,* vol. 1 (1902), 32–70.

Topping, E. S. *Chronicles of the Yellowstone.* Saint Paul, MN: Pioneer Press Publishing, 1888.

Tracy, Sarah. *A Trip Through Yellowstone.* Manuscript in the Museum of the Rockies, Bozeman, Montana.

Trumbull, Walter. "The Washburn Yellowstone Expedition." *Overland Monthly*, vol. 6 (May–June 1871): 431–37, 489–96.

Victor, Frances Fuller. *Eleven Years in the Rocky Mountains and Life on the Frontier*. Hartford, CT: Columbian Book Co., 1877.

Weikert, Andrew J. "Journal of the Tour Through the Yellowstone National Park in August and September 1877." *Contributions to the Historical Society of Montana*, vol. 3 (1900), 153–74.

Wheeler, Olin D. *Nathaniel Pitt Langford: The Vigilante, The Explorer and First Superintendent of Yellowstone Park*. Minnesota Historical Society, 1915.

PERIODICALS

Avant Courier [Bozeman, Montana]

Helena [Montana] *Weekly Herald*

Helena [Montana] *Daily Herald*

The New Northwest [Deer Lodge, Montana]

Montana, the Magazine of Western History

New Northwest

New York Times

Overland Monthly

Rocky Mountain Weekly Gazette [Helena, Montana]

Scribner's Monthly

Western Monthly

INDEX

A

Alum Creek, 60

American Fur Company, 3, 127

Antelope Creek, 40, 42

B

Baker, Major Eugene, 31

Baker, Sergeant William A., 26

Bannack, Montana, 17, 22

Barlow, Captain John W.,
    115, 139

Baronett, Jack, xi, 28, 29, 95, 96,
    142, 144, 145

Battle of the Bear Paw, 137

Bean, Elwood, 25

Beehive, the (geyser), 104

Belknap, General W. W., 131,
    139, 144

Big Cub (geyser), 103

Big Hole River, 132

Blackfeet Indians, 3, 16, 26

Blaine, James G., 113

Bottler, Frederick, 8, 9, 12, 29,
    36, 38, 40, 41, 91, 128, 129,
    131, 134

Bozeman, Montana, vii, 12, 17, 26,
    28, 31, 32, 96, 117, 128, 130,
    131, 141

Bridger, Jim, 5, 6, 18, 100

Brown Mountain, 86, 87, 97

Bullock, Seth, 119, 127, 128

C

Camp Comfort, 45

Carpenter, Frank, 133, 134

Cascade Creek, 51, 52

Castle (geyser), 103, 125

Central Pacific Railroad, 115

Cheyenne Indians, 17, 35,
    137, 140

Chief Joseph, 137

Chittenden, Hiram, 139

Civil War, 6, 8, 18, 25, 26, 61,
    129, 132

Clagett, William H., 119,
    120, 144

Clark, William, 2

Clawson, Calvin, 127

Cleveland, Grover, 143

Cody, Buffalo Bill, 131

Cole, Cornelius, 120

Colter, John, 2

Columbia River, 14

Continental Divide, 5, 9, 98, 133

Cook, Charles W., 1, 2, 11, 12, 27,
    29, 120

Cooke City, Montana, 144

Cooke, Jay, 16

Cowan, Emma, 6, 133, 134
Cowan, George, 133, 134
Craig, Montana, 144
Cross, Captain Robert, 129
Crow Indians, 2, 8, 16, 35, 36, 95, 140
Crow Reservation, 11, 17, 36
Crystal Cascade, 51
Crystal Falls, 51, 52
Curiosity Point, 64
Custer, Colonel George Armstrong, 140

D

Dawes, Henry L., 121, 122
Deadwood, South Dakota, 127
Deer Lodge, Montana, x, 8, 22, 127
DeLacy, Walter Washington, 9, 10, 11, 29
Delano, Columbus, 125
Devil's Den, 51
Dietrich, Richard, 135, 136, 137
Doane, Gustavus Cheney, vii, viii, ix, xi, 26, 28, 32, 34, 36, 39, 40, 41, 42, 45, 47, 48, 49, 50, 51, 52, 55, 56, 57, 59, 62, 63, 64, 65, 66, 68, 69, 79, 85, 86, 87, 88, 90, 91, 92, 93, 97, 103, 107, 108, 115, 116, 119, 120, 131, 138, 139, 140, 141, 145, 146
Doane, Mary Hunter, 141
Dunraven Pass, 134

E

Earl of Dunraven, the, 4, 9, 131
East Gallatin River, 32
Electric Peak, 9
Emigrant Gulch, 8, 37
Everts, Elizabeth, 142
Everts, Truman, xi, 14, 20, 22, 24, 25, 28, 39, 45, 59, 69, 70, 71, 72, 73, 74, 75, 76, 77, 78, 79, 80, 81, 82, 83, 85, 86, 87, 88, 90, 91, 93, 94, 95, 96, 97, 98, 105, 109, 111, 112, 113, 120, 141, 142, 144
Everts, Truman, Jr., 142
Excelsior Geyser, 105

F

Falls of the Yellowstone, 11, 28, 50, 51, 54, 57
Fantail (geyser), 103
Ferris, Warren Angus, 3, 4, 127
Firehole Basin, 9
Firehole River, 3, 20, 66, 97, 98, 100, 103, 104, 105, 106, 107, 134
First Peoples Mountain, 141
Folsom, David, 2, 11, 12, 13, 20, 29, 120
Fort Benton, 22, 125
Fort Bowie, 140
Fort Ellis, vii, 17, 26, 28, 31, 32, 34, 37, 42, 95, 108, 115, 130, 131, 132, 133, 140
Fort Laramie Treaty, 8, 17

G

Gallatin City, Montana, 31
Gallatin River, 3, 31, 35
Gardner River, 8, 12, 29, 38,
    39, 40
George, Yankee Jim, 130
Geronimo, 140
Giantess, the (geyser), 103, 104
Giant, the (geyser), 103
Gibbon River, 20, 106, 107
Gillette, Warren, xi, xii, 22, 28, 32,
    34, 36, 37, 41, 48, 59, 69, 85,
    86, 88, 89, 90, 91, 93, 94, 95,
    97, 142
Grand Canyon of the Colorado, ix
Grand Canyon of the Yellowstone,
    5, 8, 11, 39, 48, 49, 50, 55, 57,
    126, 135
Grand Geysers, 28, 66, 97, 98
Grand Prismatic Spring, 105
Grant, Ulysses S., 18, 24, 99, 122,
    127, 128, 131, 143, 144, 145
Grasshopper Creek, 9
Great Fountain (geyser), 105
Grotto, the (geyser), 103
Gunnison, Lieutenant John W.,
    5, 6
Guy House (hotel), 32

H

Haines, Aubrey, 125, 143
Half Way House (inn), 31
Hancock, Major General
    Winfield S., 16

Hauser, Samuel Thomas, 22, 23,
    24, 34, 35, 37, 41, 45, 47, 56,
    57, 85, 86, 88, 90, 91, 93,
    108, 143
Hayden Expedition, 112, 116,
    117, 118, 123
Hayden, F. V., 9, 113, 114, 115,
    116, 118, 119, 120, 121,
    139, 141
Hayden Valley, 65
Haynes, Jack, 106
Heap, David P., 139
Heart Lake, 140
Heart River, 140
Hedges, Cornelius, x, xi, 20, 21,
    32, 36, 40, 41, 42, 44, 50, 60,
    61, 63, 64, 69, 71, 86, 87, 92,
    98, 99, 100, 104, 105, 106,
    111, 120, 143
Helena Herald, x
Helena, Montana, 1, 2, 20, 22, 31,
    41, 69, 82, 86, 87, 94, 95, 96,
    113, 128, 133, 134, 137, 141,
    142, 143, 144
Helena Party, 135
Hell Broth Springs, 50
Henrys Lake, Idaho, 8, 30, 126,
    133, 137, 138
Horr, Harry, 121, 137

J

Jackson, William Henry, 115, 119
Jefferson River, 3, 31, 35, 117
Johnny (cook), 26, 109
Johnson, Andrew, 18

K

Kenck, Charles, 136, 137

L

Lamar River, 144
Lamar Valley, 11
Langford, Nathaniel P., vii, ix, x,
    xi, xii, 16, 17, 18, 20, 24, 25,
    30, 31, 33, 34, 35, 36, 37, 40,
    41, 42, 44, 45, 47, 49, 50, 51,
    52, 55, 56, 57, 59, 60, 61, 62,
    63, 64, 65, 66, 67, 68, 69, 79,
    85, 86, 87, 88, 91, 92, 93, 95,
    97, 98, 99, 100, 101, 105, 106,
    107, 108, 109, 111, 112, 113,
    118, 119, 120, 122, 123, 124,
    125, 126, 130, 132, 137, 138,
    139, 143, 145, 146
Lewis and Clark Expedition, 2
Lincoln, Abraham, 24
Link, Amelia, 26
Lioness, the (geyser), 103
Lion, the (geyser), 103
Lisa, Manuel, 2
Little Cub (geyser), 103
Livingston, Montana, 125, 129
Lower Falls, 28, 51, 52, 53, 54, 60,
    126, 127, 135
Lower Geyser Basin, 9, 11, 105,
    126, 127, 129, 133, 138

M

Madison Range, 79, 80
Madison River, vii, ix, 1, 3, 6, 7,
    15, 20, 29, 31, 35, 69, 78, 80,
    81, 94, 98, 106, 107, 108, 111,
    113, 114, 117, 133, 145, 146
Madison River Valley, 78
Mammoth Hot Springs, 12, 39,
    117, 121, 123, 125, 126,
    128, 130, 133, 134, 135, 136,
    137, 138
Marias Massacre, 26, 141
Marias River, 26
Mary Mountain Trail, 128
Masonic Order, 143
McCartney, James, 121, 135,
    136, 137
McCartney's Hotel, 130
McConnell, Private George, 28,
    55, 56, 57
McGuirk, Matthew, 123
Meagher, Thomas Francis, 20, 120
Meek, Joe, 3
Middle Geyser Basin, 11
Midway Geyser basin, 105
Minnesota Historical Society, 145
Missouri Pacific Railroad, 24
Missouri River, 2, 6, 22, 31, 125,
    133, 144
Montana Historical Society, 143
Montana Masonic Lodges, 31
Moore, Private Charles, 26, 28,
    93, 94
Moran, Thomas, 112, 115, 119
Mount Doane, 141
Mount Langford, 67
Mount Washburn, 49
Mud Volcano, xii, 62, 63

N

New York, New York, 16, 25

Nez Perce Creek, 134

Nez Perce Indians, 35, 132, 133, 134, 135, 136, 137, 140, 144

Norris Geyser Basin, 3

Norris, Philetus, 3, 8, 9, 12, 14, 29, 123, 138

Northern Pacific Railroad, xi, 14, 16, 112, 113, 115, 118, 121, 123, 125, 138

Nute (cook), 26, 47

O

Ogden, Utah, 115

Old Faithful, 101, 102, 125, 133

Omohundro, Texas Jack, 131

Oregon Trail, 17

Osmond, Mabel Cross, 129, 130

P

Panic of 1873, 113

Paradise Valley, 8, 12, 29, 35, 37, 128, 131

Peterson, William, 11, 29, 115, 120

Pomeroy, Samuel Clarke, 119, 120

Potts, Benjamin, 137

Potts, Daniel T., 3

Powell, John Wesley, ix

Presidio, the, 140

Pritchett, George, xi, 95, 96

R

Radersburg, Montana, 31, 133

Radersburg Party, 133, 134

Raymond, Rossiter, 30, 126, 127

Raynolds, Captain William F., 6

Raynolds Pass, 133

Reno, Major Marcus, 140

Reynolds, Charles, 25

Rhett, Minnie, 47

Roosevelt, Theodore, 127

Russell, Osborne, 4

S

Saint Paul, Minnesota, 16, 115, 145

San Francisco, California, 140, 143

Sawtell, Gilman, 8, 9, 29, 30, 126, 137, 138

Sheepeater Band of Shoshone Indians, 87, 92

Sheepeater Indians, 11

Sheridan, General Philip, 115, 136, 144

Sherman, General William Tecumseh, 132

Shively, John, 136

Shoshone Lake, 11, 98

Sioux Indians, 16, 17, 32, 35, 76, 137, 140

Sitting Bull, 137, 140

Smith, Jacob Ward, 25, 33, 34, 35, 37, 40, 41, 42, 49, 51, 57, 64, 69, 86, 87, 92, 93, 105, 106, 108, 143

Smith, Jedidiah, 5

Smithsonian Institution, 112, 115, 120, 139
Snake River, 9, 78, 91, 94, 98, 139, 140, 141
Springfield, Illinois, 24, 144
Stickney, Benjamin, 25, 41, 45, 56, 57, 86, 106, 108, 144
Stone, Emma, 128, 129
Stone, Hiram, 128
Strong, W. E., 144
Stuart, Granville, 17
Stuart, James, 17

T
Targhee Pass, 133
Tetons (mountain range), 47, 49, 64, 79
Topping, E. S., 129
Tower Creek, 42, 44, 48
Tower Fall, 11, 42, 43, 47, 133
Tracy, Sarah, 130
Tracy, W. H., 130
Trail Creek, 8, 35
Trumbull, Lyman, 24, 120, 144
Trumbull, Walter, xi, 24, 32, 41, 42, 47, 53, 85, 86, 87, 100, 101, 103, 104, 108, 112, 120, 144
Two Ocean Pass, 5

U
Union Pacific Railroad, 115, 125
Upper Basin, 100, 101, 111
Upper Falls, 52, 53, 54, 60, 126, 127, 135

Upper Geyser Basin, 3, 5, 94, 100, 101, 102, 104, 106, 126, 127, 128, 133, 134
Upper Yellowstone, 3, 4, 9, 14, 95
US Army Corps of Engineers, 138
US Army Corps of Topographical Engineers, 5
Utah and Northern Railway, 143

V
Vicksburg, Battle of, 18
Vicksburg, Mississippi, 26
Victor, Frances Fuller, 3
Virginia City, Montana, 6, 8, 9, 20, 22, 24, 25, 30, 109, 111, 113, 126
Virginia City, Nevada, 25

W
Warm Spring Creek, 40, 49
War of 1812, 2
Washburn, General Henry Dana, vii, x, 18, 19, 20, 26, 29, 31, 35, 47, 48, 50, 51, 53, 55, 57, 59, 62, 63, 85, 86, 87, 88, 90, 93, 95, 99, 101, 102, 104, 111, 115, 141
Washington, DC, 113, 118
Weikert, Andrew, 135, 136, 137
West Thumb, 3, 64, 69, 86, 90, 92, 98
West Thumb Geyser Basin, 3
Wilkie, Leslie, 135

Williamson, Private John, 28, 39, 93, 94

Willson, General Lester, 32

Willson, Mrs., 32

Wind River Mountain Range, 47

Y

Yankee Jim Canyon, 38, 96, 130

Yazoo City, Mississippi, 26

Yellowstone Falls, 82, 106, 118, 129

Yellowstone Lake, 2, 3, 8, 11, 28, 47, 48, 49, 63, 64, 65, 66, 68, 71, 73, 77, 78, 79, 85, 87, 88, 90, 92, 93, 105, 116, 117, 118, 126, 127, 129, 130, 134, 140, 141

Yellowstone Plateau, 139

Yellowstone River, vii, ix, 1, 2, 6, 7, 8, 9, 11, 12, 15, 17, 29, 31, 35, 36, 38, 39, 42, 44, 48, 49, 52, 61, 63, 65, 68, 81, 113, 114, 131, 134, 135, 140, 144, 145, 146

Yellowstone Valley, 17

Yellow Wolf (Indian), 134, 136

Yosemite Valley, 121

ABOUT THE AUTHOR

M. MARK MILLER IS A FIFTH-GENERATION MONTANAN WHO GREW UP ON a ranch in southwest Montana about ninety miles from Yellowstone National Park. His interest in early park travel began when he was a little boy listening to his grandmother's tales of cooking bread in hot springs and throwing red flannel underwear into geysers to tint their next eruption pink.

He worked for Montana newspapers while in college at the University of Montana. After graduating, he was a reporter and editor for newspapers in Utah and Kentucky. He earned a doctorate and became a journalism professor at the Universities of Wisconsin and Tennessee.

Miller returned home to Montana in 2003. He has been researching Yellowstone National Park history since then and has a collection of more than four hundred first-person accounts of park travel before 1923. Globe Pequot Press published his book *Adventures in Yellowstone: Early Travelers Tell Their Tales* in 2009.

Miller's articles on Yellowstone National Park and Montana history have appeared in the *Montana Quarterly*, *Big Sky Journal*, and the *Pioneer Museum Quarterly*. He lives in Bozeman, where he volunteers at the Pioneer Museum.

CPSIA information can be obtained
at www.ICGtesting.com
Printed in the USA
BVHW080514231221
624481BV00003B/12